W9-CPB-358

JOURNEY
FOR THE HEART

ELIZABETH A. MITCHELL

Copyright © 2008 by Elizabeth Mitchell

Awana Edition 2009

Published by Elite Publishing House
Boca Raton, FL

All rights reserved. No part of this publication may be reproduced, stored in a retrieval system or transmitted, in any form, or by any means, electronic, mechanical, recorded, photocopied, or otherwise, without the prior permission of the copyright owner, except by a reviewer who may quote brief passages in a review.

Scripture quotations used in this book are from the The Holy Bible, New International Version (NIV). Copyright 1973, 1978, 1984, International Bible Society. Used by permission of Zondervan Bible Publishers.

Printed in the United States of America

ISBN: 978-0-578-02464-6

To my husband Bill,
who honors me with sacrificial love
through every portion of our journey.

CONTENTS

Preface for the Awana Edition

JAMES SHOULD HAVE BEEN a wimpy kid. He should have been irritable, mean-spirited, and self-centered. No one would have faulted him for acting selfish or grumpy, for feeling timid or anxious. By the age of four he had endured two open heart surgeries and a myriad of procedures, transfusions, biopsies, and pacemakers. The repercussions of his second open heart surgery alone were a drug-induced coma, a five-day assault by a life-support device, and a stroke that knocked off his left side's capabilities. Any one of those might have eliminated contentment from his character. But they couldn't!

He had come wired with the capacity to shine in spite of dismal reports. This boy was packed with a resilience that no surgical trauma, annoying tray of medications, or tedious hospital stays could eliminate. The Creator developed in him the ability to endure and to overcome. Even though his body was under constant attack, his spirit flourished and prospered regardless.

In a phrase, James lived passionately. He simply thrived. Gulping the daily fist-full of pills, he accepted the rigmarole of tedious transplant management like a cowboy enthralled with the bucking bronco beneath him. He held on for the ride, hollering at top lung capacity. This bull could not get the better of him.

How did he bloom in such a precarious place? What prescription for joy did our son internalize? For one thing, he purposely kept his pity parties brief, learning along the way that no one likes attending those any way. Besides, exciting events like his weekly, action-packed Awana club meetings crowded out any wasted time spent feeling the least bit sorry for himself.

Somehow James never allowed his own limitations to block the view of others' needs. Despite prolonged physical therapy, his left hand's fine motor skills never returned after the stroke, and his torso bore over twenty different surgical scars. But James never seemed preoccupied with his weaknesses. People mattered, and rather than being self-conscious, he grew to be other-conscious. Once a friend slipped into class with a new pair of glasses perched on his nose. I later learned that David was afraid of the ridicule he might receive when his classmates saw the new addition to his face. But the first person to spot him was James. "Those are the coolest glasses I've ever seen, David," bellowed James. No one mentioned the glasses after that.

Perhaps because James had received huge quantities of love from so many on his life adventures, he returned the favor by loving others unconditionally. In almost every group picture with James, his right arm is locked around somebody's neck in an enormous hug. All fifteen cousins thought they were James' favorite and all four aunts secretly believed he preferred their cooking. He took his designation as a "Leader-in-Training" at Awana seriously, and the boys under his care distinctly knew James was on their side, cheering for them at handbook and game time, celebrating their every attempt to hide the treasure of God's Word in their hearts.

Gratefulness marked his days more significantly than any scar across his chest and made ordinary events a full-blown celebration. A fist-full of Awana bucks and ten minutes of store-time and life was simply grand. Thankfulness spilled from him as if he fully comprehended that his very life was a gift and anything, anything at all, that was tacked onto a day, was worthy of appreciation. The word "best" resonated through his vocabulary and spurted out frequently in conversations. Those were the "best" cookies he ever ate, that was certainly the "best" Awana Grand Prix race he had ever attended, and the three-pointer in his basketball game was most definitely the "best" one he ever made.

In some respects, James attacked every task that crossed his day as if his very life depended on its success. Vacuuming was a race to beat yesterday's time. Schoolwork was an obstacle to scale faster and more furiously than the previous day. Basketball games drew out the champion inside him, and he threw himself into them like they were all-star televised events. Memorizing Awana verses was a vigorous challenge to be met with fierce, unwavering determination. He couldn't help it! Enormous gallons of competitive energy surged through him and he erupted enthusiastically regardless of the routine setting. Nothing seemed like a trivial pursuit for James.

On Wednesday nights he sprinted out of our car with the other eight children from our neighborhood that came with him to Awana, racing them down the cement path at full speed towards his TNT room. He wore his bright, green shirt with pride and spent time locked in his room almost every Wednesday afternoon working on the handbook sections with his cousin Austin. Our son received his Timothy Award as if accepting the Nobel Peace Prize for Grand Accomplishments, and proudly displayed it by his bed with his most favorite treasures. He memorized the names of all the books in the Old and New Testament, winning a prize on Talent Night for being able to rip through them in perfect order in less than 12 seconds flat.

Somehow, he was able to convert the mundane into explosive excitement. During his turn at family-night games, he slammed down each piece with an audible thud as his palm slapped the kitchen table. Those 1000-piece jigsaw puzzles failed to overwhelm because he kept a running tally on the number of pieces placed rather than focusing on the jumbled pile before him. Rides in the car were habitually converted into intense competitions to see who could accumulate the highest points by being the first to spot particular types of vehicles before returning to our driveway. He dashed around the game circle at Awana like an Olympic contender, relishing every opportunity to grab that orange baton from center square. One September he scribbled a note and held it up for posterity, "I am done my first day of school and only 179 more to go." The camera captured that moment and in the picture James wears a smile big enough for ten ordinary folk. That was his signature always.

To trace James' life is to follow a trail of passionate joy. What was the source of this free-flowing delight that spilled over the banks of his life? In a word --relationships. God placed James in our family with dozens of cousins, aunts, uncles, siblings, and grandparents to reinforce him on every side. For each of us, James was a courier from heaven, a constant reminder that God is good and does all things well. We got to love James. He loved us back. We were knitted tightly together, taught strands made by way of hardships and healings. Like "Gorilla Glue," we forged an unbreakable bond through fiery rescue operations. James flourished amidst all those wonderful relationships and responded to life atop that secure, loving platform.

But even more significantly, James had an intimate relationship with his Creator. At the age of five, sitting beside me on our family-room couch, he surrendered his life to the Lord and began his own earthly pilgrimage hand in hand with the One who knew him best of all. We encouraged him to read biographies of great men and women of faith and he learned of passionate perseverance and steadfast obedience from their examples. Because saints like Amy Carmichael and George Mueller kept careful records of God's work in their lives, I encouraged James to keep his own journal. In the fall of 2002 he wrote, "God is so big…so powerful too. He's a great God, that's why he's my God." Truth internalized.

Awana was instrumental in encouraging in James a deep love for God's Word and developing in him an uncanny ability to memorize great chunks of Scripture. We challenged our children to read through the Bible in one year and James met that goal twice. Through the partnership between our church, home school community, extended family, and his Awana leaders, God was about preparing James for heaven. As parents we take seriously the need to prepare our children for school, camp, college and eventually marriage. We have a sense of satisfaction when they reach their destination with all the requirements fulfilled. When James entered heaven, he had the Savior in his heart and the Scriptures planted in his soul. We had taught him about his Heavenly Father, he had an intimate relationship with Jesus Christ, and he had studied with us the wonderful stories in Scripture. It gave me great joy to realize that as James would encounter Moses, Abraham, or Joseph, they would be familiar friends because he had learned much about them while he lived on earth.

Sometimes we foolishly believe that a trouble-free life is a mark of God's blessing and favor, but the Bible repeatedly proves that theory inaccurate. Actually, Joseph's life in the book of Genesis demonstrated the opposite reality. While he was a slave in a foreign land, while he was hundreds of miles away from his father and his homeland, he was falsely accused and thrown into a wretched prison dungeon. But even there, precisely there, Genesis 39 and 40 repeatedly tell us, "The Lord was with Joseph and he prospered." God had a job for Joseph in the midst of adversity. The difficulties were preparation for him to be radically transformed and to dramatically affect his world. "But while Joseph was there in the prison, the Lord was with Him." Joseph learned the invaluable lesson that God's presence and His favor are gracious, good gifts that He bestows on His children regardless of their immediate circumstances.

In some ways, James' life is an example of a modern day Joseph. As God stood beside James and enabled him to endure immense hardship, all who knew him were aware that "The Lord was with him." God created James as a remarkable young man who reflected the unchanging truth that His grace is sufficient and made perfect in the weakest of vessels.

CHAPTER 1

A GOD-SIZE EMERGENCY

"I will try to always trust in the Lord, I will never be afraid or terrified because I know the Lord will never leave me."

— James' Journal Entry, March 4, 2005

THE metallic bird crouched on the steamy asphalt pad like an enormous vulture, eagerly anticipating its prey. Within minutes it would lift off from the heliport at Miami Children's Hospital and separate us from everyone familiar, from everything safe, reasonable or fair. The paramedics lifted the gurney, locked its wheels in place and adjusted our son's intravenous lines as I cautiously climbed inside this alien machine dragging duffle bags and a borrowed suitcase along. I had quickly packed our meager hospital belongings while the orange-clad transport team prepared James for his six hour flight to Gainesville in north Florida. Our hope hung precariously on the helicopter blades; our son's heart was hanging by a thread.

"Are you OK, Buddy?" I asked looking into his chocolate brown eyes, rimmed with gray circles. Four-year-old James flashed me a sleepy half-smile and quickly gave me a thumbs-up motion. "Don't be scared, OK? We're just off on another adventure. Daddy will fly on a plane and meet us later."

"Not scared, Mom. No way. Isn't this helicopter awesome?"

I swallowed the lump in my throat. "You're the one who's awesome, Jamers. I'm just glad I get to be here with you."

How could I be anywhere else? Our son's battery had suddenly run out and his frail body was marked by every physical symptom of a geriatric cardiac patient. His zipper-scarred chest covered a worn pump that chugged pathetically from four years of front line assault. Incapable of continuing the fight, his heart had simply waved its white flag of surrender.

The paramedics monitored his support system, checked the intravenous lines, and pumped in more medications; I leaned forward and fingered his limp hair. The sunlit tones now drooped dimly, exposing patches of bald spots, visible reminders of drug-induced comas on by-pass machines that caused strokes. I caressed his skinny arms, colored by needle bruises and plastic hospital identification bracelets, and grasped his shoulder as I felt the giddy sensation of the helicopter's rapid ascent.

"Put these on," the paramedics urged, handing me large headphones to block out the engine's enormous clamor. I slipped them on quickly, eager to ask, "What can you give me to alleviate this pounding in my chest?" I stifled the urge to scream by biting hard on my lower lip. Our son was dying. We flew in haste to find a heart he could call his own.

The medication quickly made James unconscious and his peaceful face resembled a child simply lulled to sleep within the arms of an enormous rocking chair. But where was my sleeping potion? Parents on emergency helicopter airlifts should have pills too. I turned to stare out the window, my pulse pounding in my ears, my throat parched. From our elevation of three thousand feet, the familiar landscape was strangely altered. The grand hotels and glass-encased office complexes appeared as insignificant childish models; the super highways were a jumble of black threads scattered randomly in a field.

In a way, our life had become a jumble of black threads randomly scattered in a landscape of underground land mines where bombs frequently, unexpectedly detonated our world. With each successive explosion, with each shattering diagnosis, we were forced to undergo the tremors of war. And now we had embarked on the most difficult campaign. After four-and-a-half years of scrambling through surgeries, procedures, doctors, surgeons, specialists, ambulances and incisions, the medical consensus was grim - a heart transplant was the only option available. Every other avenue would literally be a dead-end.

Death always lingered close and invariably stuck its grotesque face into our family portraits. We tried desperately to flee, to hide from its evil smile, but it pursued us relentlessly, sneering cruelly at our family gatherings. For brief spells we escaped, relaxed our defenses, and then were horrified when death slinked back into the picture. To gaze now at James' scrawny frame beneath the hospital blanket, to see the outline of pencil-thin legs and protruding collar bone was to view that menacing figure close at hand.

The helicopter's rapid descent startled both of us, and his eyelids fluttered open as we landed on the roof of the eleven-story Shands Hospital at the University of Florida. The transport team unlocked the wheels, lifted the gurney down and barreled through the first set of electronic doors. Rapidly, they pushed his gurney down corridors, around corners, into an elevator, through doorways, past nurses' stations and into the Pediatric Cardiac Intensive Care Unit (CICU). They were expecting us.

"Mrs. Mitchell, I am Dr. Jay Fricker." The Chief Pediatric Cardiologist and the Medical Director of Pediatric Heart Transplants bent down and shook our little boy's hand as if he were meeting a dignitary. His eyes were kind and a full beard surrounded a warm smile as he continued, "And this must be James."

"Oh, yes," I said. "This is world famous James Mitchell."

"Well, I know how famous he is. I already know James."

"You do? We didn't think we knew anyone at this hospital."

"Six weeks ago you and your husband spoke at the Cardiac Symposium in Palm Beach and shared the trauma of pediatric cardiac surgery from a family's perspective," said Dr. Fricker. "I was one of the hundred doctors in the audience who heard James' story and saw him on stage. You don't know me, but I already know much about you."

Dr. Fricker fixed his gaze on his tiny patient. "So, you see, James, we're friends already." I felt instantly at peace.

During the course of two hours, six different specialists walked into our new home, a glass-encased isolation room immediately in front of the nurse's station. Each one shook James' hand, stated his area of expertise, and warmed his stethoscope with his palm before lightly placing it over our son's heart. "James Mitchell, what a pleasure to meet you. I am one of the doctors here at Shands. I am going to do all I can to help you. Do you have any questions for me?" We heard six different variations with the same theme.

James pulled the back of his hair up through the fingers of his right hand and stared into each new face while he rested on his sage green pillow. He tolerated their presence without saying one word, without muttering one whimper. We were both strangers in a new land, refugees seeking asylum from the tyranny of a broken heart, and yet, somehow, we felt safe. I stood guard beside James' bed; God's peaceful presence stood guard within me. It was apparent we were exactly where He wanted us.

By the time my husband Bill arrived at the Gainesville airport and taxied over to join us, Dr. Fricker and his team had meticulously examined James' records, CAT scans, X-rays and echocardiograms. With each test result, Dr. Fricker's smile had drained from his face, and he now carefully measured each of his words. "Kelli Harker is our transplant coordinator. She'll organize all the details for the transplant. She's the one who will answer your questions and help resolve any difficulties. Tomorrow she'll place James on the National Organ Transplant Registry. Of course, he will have to stay at the hospital, connected to the intravenous medications. In some cases, our patients are permitted to remain at home with monitoring and be called immediately when a compatible heart is found. I'm afraid this just isn't possible in James' case."

"Dr. Fricker," I asked. "Is he permitted to get out of bed?"

"As a precaution, I'd rather he just stay put."

"How long do you think we'll be here?" Bill asked.

"Well, that's hard to say," Dr. Fricker replied. "James has a slight advantage, in one sense, in that his present heart is so significantly enlarged that he probably could be matched to a donor much older than him. As you can imagine, there are a lot more incidents of adult donors than children James' age."

We could imagine many things. But, instead, we fed James dinner, found a stash of videos he enjoyed, prepared him for bed, and held his hand until he fell asleep. We gave all our phone numbers to the nurse, walked across the highway, found a hotel room and showered away the grime of the day. Late into the night, my imagination danced wildly as my eyelids refused to close and cover the maddening thoughts spinning like helicopter blades. *How had we ended up in this strange place once more? Hadn't we been in far too many strange places in his four-and-a-half years? What sort of journey was still ahead? Could we do this one more time?* It was January 15, 1998 and we had traveled far, but not, it seemed, nearly far enough.

At the outset of this treacherous expedition, in the early morning hours of March 23, 1993, I remember waking to the wretched realization that my arms ached from emptiness; our newborn son would soon be forced to run away from home. I should have been propped up in the maternity ward, cradled between clean, crisp sheets, a queen awaiting audience with her fourth-born. But he was never introduced. Instead, the nurses relayed vague explanations from their cubicles. "He's too cold. We will bring him down to you when he's warm." It gradually dawned on us that we would freeze beneath the paralyzing chill of the unknown.

I yearned to envelope him close, to press his chubby face against mine and inhale his sweetness. The smooth delivery had gone fast, the easiest of my four births, and we had no reason to be alarmed. He weighed nine and a half pounds and the pediatrician had given him a clean bill of health. As they wheeled me out of the delivery room I spotted his pediatrician, Dr. Jack Blanco, in the hallway.

"How is James?" I called out.

"All's well. He has a slight crimp in his right ear, but nothing to worry about. No baby's perfect."

How perfect! Bill walked beside my bed, and we smiled, anticipating introducing James to his big brothers Billy and Gregory and his sister Jacqui. As soon as we were settled in the maternity suite we would ask their grandmother Mimi to bring them over to meet James.

But he never came. Instead, a pale blue uniformed woman marched through the doorway. "Mrs. Mitchell. I am the neonatologist."

I cannot remember her name, but I will never forget those words. "Is anything wrong?" I pleaded, springing off the starched white sheets as if stung by her introduction.

"There might be," she replied, her words unraveling every fiber of our world.

There would be hours of waiting while numbing uncertainty paraded around my bed and pressed itself against my chest. The Neonatal Intensive Care Unit (NICU) called in a pediatric cardiologist to assess James. His color was dusky; the level of oxygen in his blood dangerously low.

"I knelt beside the empty cradle and prayed before racing back here," Bill whispered. He reached out his hand and tenderly brushed back my damp hair. But we did not speak; all our words evaporated in the haze.

Into our dilemma walked Dr. Joelle Miller. At four in the afternoon of the longest day we had ever experienced, we met with her in a cramped consultation room. She spared the small talk and with concise terms and simple sketches detailed our son's complex condition.

"James has congenital heart disease," Dr. Miller began. "His main defect is transposition of the great arteries." I wrapped the thin bathrobe tighter around my swollen stomach; the temperature had suddenly dropped.

"Before you realized you were pregnant, while his heart was being formed in its microscopic proportion, his two main arteries developed in reverse, directly opposite to how they are normally connected. The blood supplied with oxygen is being inadvertently pumped back to the lungs instead of out to the rest of his body. Conversely, the deoxygenated blood is never routed to his lungs. The main supply of oxygen-starved blood is pulsing through his body carrying a deathly low level of oxygen."

I leaned forward, wanting to turn Dr. Miller off like an offensive television show, but I was incapable of changing the channel. The grotesque reality show only intensified.

"James also has atrial septal defects and ventricle septal defects," she continued. "These are tears or holes in the linings between his upper and lower chambers. In both these abnormalities, blood returning to the heart from the lungs is short-circuited and sent back to the lungs rather than pumped to the rest of the body. From the echocardiogram it appears his mitral valve is also deformed."

I could not be hearing correctly. This stranger could not possibly be referring to our baby. I glanced over at Bill's drained expression and knew our life was ebbing away, slowly seeping away until nothing normal could remain.

Dr. Miller completed her appraisal. "None of the hospitals in Florida have the experience to deal with his condition. Children's Hospital in Boston would be my first choice. Philadelphia Children's Hospital my second. They're the only places with the medical teams experienced enough with repairing transpositions."

When the room vibrated with the details of air ambulances, insurance coverage and Bill joining the transport team for the emergency flight to Boston, I fled. I returned to bed, pulled up the blanket and faced the wall. The pastel colors and quaint paintings in the maternity suite sneered back. I had foolishly prepared for our new baby for nothing. I couldn't even touch him, or nurse him or anything.

Icy fear-filled waves descended, sucking me underneath the foam, flinging me upside down, everything upside down. The sea water swirled over my head; the salt saturated my mouth while the waves slapped me, stifled me, forced me down. I wanted to vomit, to purge the sickening lump lodged deep inside. I was drowning with no buoy in sight, no hand to grasp and wrench me out of this wretched place. What would we do now? Who could possibly help us now?

"Help us, Father," I prayed with my face pressed into the pillow.

"Help us now. We need you now." From a distant place I vaguely heard my sisters calling our family and friends to prayer. I, too, should be making phone calls, sitting up and calling someone to help. But the freeze was unyielding.

Finally, I turned to face my younger sister. "Read the Psalms for me."

She reached for the Bible, fingered the pages and began with Psalm 27. "The Lord is my light and my salvation, whom shall I fear? The Lord is the stronghold of my life, of whom shall I be afraid?" From within the waves' embrace I heard her continue, "When evil men advance against me to devour my flesh, when my enemies and my foes attack me, they will stumble and fall."

Cautiously, I rose to the surface. "Though an army besiege me, my heart will not fear, though war break out against me, even then will I be confident." The familiar verses fit like a life-jacket and as she continued reading those ancient words, songs penned in pits of despair and disaster, I rested with the taste of fresh water washing away the salt.

When the NICU called, I scurried down the corridor, scrubbed my hands, and slipped on a hospital gown. James' bags were packed, his ticket purchased and the waving gallery open for farewells. He looked beautiful even beneath the coiled intravenous lines and oxygen tubes, and my tears began again. Soon they dripped off the tip of my nose like rainwater off a beaten-down roof.

Perhaps if I could hold him, press him to my breast and cradle him close. Perhaps if I could ...but I could just touch him, breathe his name and cry quietly to the Creator of the universe. It was apparent He was in charge; I was not. The NICU grew still and I no longer noticed the commotion of the nurses checking their tiny charges. My eyes rested on James, but the harsh hand of fright began to loosen its hold. In the way I yearned to help James, God longed to help me. As I desired to hold my child, I felt the Lord holding me. While I bent close to whisper my love into James' ear, my Heavenly Father whispered to me, "Fear not... you are mine. When you pass through the waters, I will be with you and when you pass through the rivers, they will not sweep over you"

(Isaiah 43:1-2). That's right. I was passing through the waters, but I was not passing through alone. He was beside me even in this despicable situation. A cotton blanket covered James and an indescribable peace covered me. Gradually, I felt warm.

Hadn't the Lord promised to be my stronghold right in the middle of the siege, and wasn't He calling Himself my salvation precisely because I needed rescuing? If I allowed Him, His presence, and not fear, would cling tightly to me. I could trust Him. He had always proven Himself to be fully and completely trustworthy. Those verses were not sweet fairy tales or simple childhood beliefs. No. They were life and hope a loving Father poured into a mother's broken heart. For He, more than any other, knew exactly how it felt to have a wounded son.

I slipped out of the NICU, slipped my arms around Billy and Greg who had been waiting outside the door, and left James behind.

CHAPTER 2

COMFORT IN THE SKY

"God wants us to listen to what he says and listen to his words."
-James' Journal Entry, September 17, 2004

I t was the cats that made me cry.

They stood guard, strays in assorted shades and sizes, lounging on their furry bellies by the hospital exit doors. My husband Bill and I spotted them when we left as beaming parents with our firstborn son Billy, in July 1984. To us they were Bethesda Memorial Hospital's unofficial mascots who waved their tails in a 21-gun salute as Bill escorted me to our car. They greeted us as we paraded out proudly three years later with Gregory and when we departed triumphantly with Jacqueline in February of 1990, I smiled as we sailed past their waving gallery.

But today we carried no cameras, no diaper bags, and no baby. I glanced at the cats, felt the heaviness of vacant arms and slumped into my mother-in-law's car for the drive to her home.

"Is it only Wednesday, Mom? Has only one day passed since James was born?"

"Tell me what you heard from Bill," she coaxed.

"The airplane landed in the snow," I began. "A siren-screeching ambulance drove them at 100 miles an hour to Boston Children's. Teams of doctors have been in James' cubicle all morning. They confirmed everything our cardiologist told us yesterday. James has a severely deformed heart. They'll do the open heart surgery in a few days."

On Thursday morning I woke in the guestroom with my limbs pretending paralysis and my brain behaving oddly. Somehow during the night, cotton balls had moved in and taken up residence and all ability to think or plan or reason had been suffocated somewhere between fuzziness and weariness. I climbed out of bed, longing to play with the other children, to bring some semblance of normalcy to their day. But I sat suddenly; unable to figure out why I had stood up in the first place. The phone rang and I heard Bill's voice. "How's James?" I asked.

"They're working on him constantly. He's in the Pediatric Cardiac ICU with his own nurse."

"What are the doctors saying?"

"That there's not a moment to spare. They've scheduled James' open heart surgery for tomorrow morning."

"Tomorrow! I thought you said they're going to assess him for a few days and consider exactly what to do."

"They decided against that. They told me every minute is vital. They've squeezed him in. He can't afford to wait any longer."

The cotton balls were not making any room for the brain cells to re-engage. "What should I do?" I asked.

"Well, if you want to be here for surgery, you need to fly into Boston today. If you wait till tomorrow, you won't be here in time." He sighed. "Do you feel strong enough to make the flight?"

No. No. Not strong enough, never strong enough for this. "I don't know. I want to be there so badly."

"Do what you think is best, sweetheart. You're the one who's just delivered a baby. I don't even know if it's safe for you to travel. Call your doctors and call me back so I know what you've decided."

Decided? Yes, I needed to decide. But why was I standing on a carousel? Why was everything moving so fast? Why couldn't someone realize he had to slow this thing down so I could climb off? I glanced down at my belly protruding as if I was still five months pregnant. It was snowing in Boston and the only warm thing I owned big enough to drape this spectacle was my fuzzy robe. Somehow, cotton balls and all, I realized that might be inappropriate travel wear.

"Lord," I whispered. "I need help".

My limbs apparently hadn't heard that prayer. "Lord, help me find a flight. Help me know what to pack. Help me tell the kids I have to leave them behind. God, I can't do this. You've got to help me. I can't even think what I need to do."

Think. I needed to think. Let me call Mom. Let me phone Kathy and Souhila. They would think for me.

Slowly, like a fog exposed to sunlight, the murkiness gradually lifted as I relayed the news. In Three Musketeer-fashion they immediately moved into action. Mom hauled out every warm outfit and ensemble she owned, piled them on the bed, maneuvered them over my pudgy shape, found a suitcase and threw in the acceptable pieces. The doorbell rang and Kathy sailed in Mary Poppins-style to distract the children. Souhila swooped in with a smile on her face and a toiletry bag at her side. She had raided her own supplies and corralled every undergarment, cosmetic and hygiene item I could ever possibly need.

I kissed and hugged the kids, swung by my parents' home to kiss and hug them, and realized our Thursday Bible Study was in full swing. I had no time to greet them but I knew they would pray me through this journey, no matter how long the trip.

Time was running out. The only available flight to Boston would soon leave without me, but I had to stop and spend a minute with my mom, sitting helpless in her wheelchair, paralyzed from a stroke. She wanted to help me; I wanted to help James. At that point, neither of us was capable of helping our child. Willing, yes; able, no.

"Mummy. I need you to be brave."

"I wish I could do something," she said as tears spilled over her face.

"You pray, Mummy. It's going to be OK. You pray us home."

My sisters and two sisters-in-law escorted me to the car and hugged me tightly. The Lion of Judah had bent his majestic frame, shaken his royal mane and breathed out His magnificent strength through my family. His breath even blew the cotton balls away.

But in gaining strength, I lost time. I raced to the airport with Bill's parents, knowing I was moments from missing my flight. The terminal bulged with a massive passenger jam and the plane would depart in 15 minutes. The line barely crept forward. I glanced at the 40 people ahead of me, slipped up the side and approached the counter.

"Excuse me, Sir," my voice trembled. "Our newborn son faces open heart surgery tomorrow. If I miss my flight, I'll miss everything. Is there anything you can do to help me?"

A lady behind me spoke loudly, "She can have my seat. Give her mine."

"Don't you worry, ma'am," he replied, punching keys on his computer. "I'll tell the pilot to hold the plane for you."

I plopped myself in a courtesy wheelchair and the attendant maneuvered me through every possible short-cut. We reached the gate and I leaped up to hug Bill's parents good-by. Mom's voice wavered. "I hate for you to get on that plane alone. How I wish I could go with you."

"Mom, you are doing the far better thing. You are taking care of the children for me."

"Elizabeth, I want you to remember," my father-in-law said as he gave me his hallmark bear hug. "There will be a day of victory. Remember, we'll have a day of victory soon."

I nodded, hurried down the ramp, collapsed into my seat and watched the flight attendant close the door behind me. I waited for turmoil and fear to press their faces against mine. They never did. I fastened the seatbelt, rested my head back and the sense of a warm, soothing blanket draped over me. Every square of this serene quilt was a shield blocking out worrisome intrusions and I settled beneath the folds conscious of God's gentle presence. Later, I would discover that hundreds of prayer warriors had knitted that blanket around me.

I ignored the clamor of the in-flight movie and chattering passengers and eased out my Bible. As I flipped it open, my eyes rested on Psalms

20. Every verse somersaulted directly into my heart beginning with the first one. *"May the Lord answer you when you are in distress." Lord, you know exactly where I am, don't you? You are speaking right to me, in the middle of this flight, in the midst of our storm. God, you are answering me in my distress.*

I continued reading. "May the name of the God of Jacob protect you. May He send you help from the sanctuary and grant you support from Zion." *Father, you are protecting James and our children. You are our protection. You are my support even now and I know you will continue to help us.*

My eyes followed the next verse eagerly. "May he give you the desire of your heart and make all your plans succeed. We will shout for joy when you are victorious and will lift up our banners in the name of our God. May the Lord grant all your requests." *Lord, I prayed silently without a thought to all the distractions around me, your voice and your promise to make our plans for James successful, is giving me such hope.*

The Psalm ended even more pleasantly than it had begun. "Some trust in chariots and some in horses, but we trust in the name of the Lord, our God."

I lay back against the padded headrest and placed my palm on the pages of my Bible. I did not need to trust in world-famous surgeons or world-renown hospitals for my help. I did not need to trust brilliant minds and professional hands to cure James. Naturally, God would use each of those. But our trust, my trust, was in the very name of God, the infinitely compassionate God who chose to direct my eyes to this specific Psalm in order to speak these specific words into my soul.

Each word drew me in like a famished soul to a feast. "...Great is his joy in the victories you give! You have granted him the desire of his heart and have not withheld the request of his lips...In you our Fathers put their trust; they trusted and you delivered them. They cried to you and were saved; in you they trusted and were not disappointed."

Father, you are promising to deliver me. You are speaking directly to me right here in my seat on a plane with all these people around oblivious to my pain. Lord, as I cry out to you, you are saving

James. I can trust you and not be disappointed. How marvelous.
You are more than I could ever imagine.

In Psalm 25 I soaked in the truth that He would show me the way, He would teach me the path to take, He would guide me and I could rest in Him all day long. I relished the flavor of each word and felt saturated to the point of bursting wide open as I read verse 12 to verse 15. "Who then is the man that fears the Lord? He will instruct him in the way chosen for him. He will spend his days in prosperity and his descendants will inherit the land. The Lord confides in those who fear Him; He makes his covenant known to them. My eyes are ever on the Lord, for only He will release my feet from the snare."

Lord, I am so moved by your tenderness. To think you would confide
in me, share your inner thoughts with me. To realize that as I keep
me eyes on you, you are the one who will release my feet from the
snares of fear, worry and weariness.

I underlined almost every verse I encountered, each one now a personal ally in the fight. With every Scripture my Father confirmed that I would see his goodness and could rest confidently in His promises. I had dialogued with the Deity thousands of feet in the air, hundreds of miles from home, without ever hearing an audible word. I had no idea then, but our intimate conversation had only just begun.

CHAPTER 3

PILLSBURY DOUGH BOYS
WEAR PACEMAKERS, TOO

"I want God to be my rock, my fortress and my deliverer."
-James' Journal Entry, April 1, 2005

O N the morning of his third day, our son faced his first open-heart surgery. A lifetime had already been ripped away from us.

When I had arrived in Boston the evening before, Bill, now familiar with the security restrictions on the sixth floor of the Pediatric CICU of Boston Children's, buzzed in to receive permission before we entered James' cubicle. The energetic, blonde nurse stationed by his bed monitored the machines and medication lines constantly. James lay on his back and looked perfectly comfortable, a diaper draped loosely over him, his bare chest covered by EKG leads. Carefully, I bent over the crib, not wanting to disconnect anything important and kissed his chubby face and the top of his perfectly shaped head. Tomorrow they would wheel him away from us, slice through his chest, cut through his sternum and attempt to reconstruct his walnut-sized heart. But for now, I could touch him still.

A parade of anesthesiologists, surgeons, cardiac specialists, nurses and technicians continually interrupted us in an attempt to educate us on the many facets of the impending six-hour surgery and recovery period.

Each one carried a small pad of paper in their palm to diagram James' precise abnormalities and a stack of consent forms requiring signatures. By the end of the consultations, I felt as if the mammoth hospital building was crammed inside my gut.

"Won't you come this way," a nurse motioned. "We want you to view a patient who underwent open-heart surgery this morning. We think it might help prepare you for what you will see when James returns from the operating room." She escorted us into a tiny cubicle and stood silently while we gaped with wide eyes and tight lips at the tiny baby. Every square inch of his body was pumped-up tight; his eyelids bulged, his lips were split open, his skin stretched taught across swollen limbs. A red incision ran from his breast bone to his belly button, while dozens of lines and tubes ran across his body as if he had been caught in a surgical spider web.

The nurse cleared her throat; we kept our eyes on the baby. "In order for the surgeons to operate on the heart, its own pulsing rhythm must be stilled. Before the surgery can occur, the patient is connected to a heart/lung machine that takes over the functions of both of these organs. The machine controls the breathing and ensures that blood continues to be pumped throughout his body. But in the process, the body absorbs volumes of fluid. This puffiness is the result," her voice trailed off.

The pressure behind my eyes, the throbbing of my engorged breasts, and the weight of a thousand unanswered questions cornered me. Like a trapped animal, my eyes darted around for an escape route. Bill had quickly toured me around the parent quarters and had shoved my suitcase into a closet before we went to see James. *Where was that room now?*

"Bill."

"Yes, Hon."

"I have to leave. Do you mind? Where's the shower? I can't seem to remember my way around."

He thanked the nurse and we left. I shuffled through my suitcase, found the toiletry bag and stumbled to the door marked "Parent Lavatory." I climbed into the tub, turned the faucets on, and let all the pressure backed up behind my eyes seep out.

* * *

It was high noon when they came for James.

I had paced around his tiny cubicle waiting for a chance to hold him and finally pulled a rocking chair right beside his small bed in anticipation. The nurse hoisted James up, untangled his tubes, and carefully placed him in my arms.

"You haven't held him since the delivery, have you?" Bill's eyes filled with tears.

I shook my head. The weight of his body felt perfect in my arms and I quickly grew accustomed to the paraphernalia connecting him to the monitors stationed around the bed. The nurse's radio peeked out from behind the computer screen and a country singer crooned out, "How Could I Ever Live Without Him." I held James tighter, rubbing my hand across his back while the tears ran down my face. *How could I ever live without him? What is God asking us to do?*

The surgical team interrupted us, and I returned James to his bed for them to prepare him for the operation. Bill held my hand as we escorted them to the elevator. James was fast asleep, and we both bent our heads towards his.

"We love you, James. We'll see you soon, Sweetie. Jesus is with you," I whispered into his tiny ear.

Before we lifted our heads, Bill prayed. "Father, protect our son. Bring him safely through this surgery. We give him to you again." The elevator closed. It would be dark before we would see him again.

We wandered to the waiting area and surprisingly were assigned a small, private room, away from the congestion. We had anticipated an excruciating six-hour wait, but, instead, calm controlled that tiny room and barred fear from entry.

"Elizabeth, we're walking through the valley and God is keeping us from fearing evil, isn't He?"

I glanced at my extremely tall husband, his long legs stretching almost to the door. "I know hundreds of people are praying for us right now.

That's why we feel His presence and His peace. Only God could do this."

An electric breast pump stood beside the couch, and I carefully extracted my milk for later feedings. With one hand I controlled the pump and with the other I turned the pages of my Bible. James would need the milk for crucial nourishment; I desperately needed the Word for survival. I returned to the Psalms, drawing oxygen into what should have been a stifling place as the truth in each phrase blew away my anxious wonderings. Journaling was impractical as I sat perched between pump and couch, and I jotted brief notes in the margin of the Bible, fully aware I was on a journey where my sanity totally depended on saturating my mind with the Truth of God's Word.

With His impeccable timing, He led me to verses which charged me with courage precisely when I needed them. At 8 that morning, after my weepy bathroom session, my eyes rested on Psalms 30:4-5 and I read, "Sing to the Lord, you saints of his…weeping may remain for a night but rejoicing comes in the morning." When we first sat in the waiting room at 12:30 p.m., I had arrived at Psalm 31:7. "I will be glad and rejoice in your love, for you saw my affliction and knew the anguish of my soul." As 4 p.m. rolled around, and we waited desperately for some news from the OR, I reached Psalm 32:6-7. "Therefore, let everyone who is Godly pray to you while you may be found; surely when the mighty waters rise, they will not reach him. You are my hiding place; you will protect me from trouble and surround me with songs of deliverance." He was protecting us, surrounding us with Himself and using the songs of the psalmists to bring us deliverance.

The surgeon opened the door of our waiting area at 5:15 p.m. We gave him our full attention.

"The surgery went reasonably well," Dr. Jonas began. "We were able to repair the transposition and the ASD and VSD. The mitral valve was such that with the length of the surgery we left it alone. The next 48 hours are critical. Everything will depend on how he recovers during this time."

He closed the door, and we closed our eyes. "Father, we are so grateful. Be with James even now. Give his body what it needs to fight and heal. Give us what we need as well." We picked up the phone and relayed the good news home, took a walk, ate dinner and returned to wait for admission to James' room.

Eight hours had passed since we had seen him, and when the nurse finally allowed us entry, we were still unprepared. A massive array of spaghetti-like wiring spilled across his small body. Three transparent tubes draining blood from his incision protruded like spears from his chest and flowed across his bed like miniature garden hoses. A catheter sneaked out from a propped-open diaper, draining urine into a large, transparent bag. Blue, temporary pacemaker wires exited his chest and zigzagged across the entire length of his bed. Wide white tape secured tubes going into his nostrils. Both his arms were strapped to boards while IV lines pumped in medications.

An incision over his right ankle bone was covered with clear tape and when we inquired the nurse explained, "In the event that the surgeons needed to immediately access a vein, they would have no trouble finding that one."

We stood silently by his bed, our eyes cross-examining the nurses as they moved incessantly. At 10:30 p.m. his cardiologist, Dr. Chang, came in.

"He's stable. Why don't you get some sleep? You're just down the hall. His nurse will get you if you're needed." We took that tiny sliver of encouragement to pack ourselves off to bed. James had made it through his grueling six-hour surgery. We laid our heads on that comforting thought and fell asleep.

The days and nights melted into each other, a mixture of waiting, watching, hoping. Nurses pumped medicines through his IV lines, measured urine output, and monitored his blood pressure, heart rate, and oxygen level. The cardiac surgical team and a medical team made rounds every morning, making notes, altering treatments, fine-tuning his diagnosis. We hung a picture of Billy, Greg and Jacqui right over his bed and their cheerful, smiling faces always brought comments as the teams evaluated James.

At one point, his swollen body bore a striking resemblance to the "Michelin Man" and the "Pillsbury Dough Boy" rolled together. We celebrated each day's successful urine output as proof his kidneys were processing the gigantic volume of medications, and felt relieved as his body gradually returned to its proper size. In the process, we began to perform routine baby tasks like feeding him breast milk from a sterilized bottle, plugging his pink lips with a pacifier, holding him and burping him without worrying about the incisions scattered all over his sturdy chest. His soft skin, his delicious smell, his chubby arms and legs were irresistible as we simply began to enjoy our newborn for the first time. We also received advice that would prove invaluable in the years ahead.

"Don't ever raise a cardiac kid," the medical teams counseled. "Don't treat him any different than you do your other kids. Let him live as normal a life as possible. Don't pamper and spoil him just because he has congenital heart disease. Let him thrive and live life to the fullest. Don't ever coddle him. You will only spoil him and ruin his life."

His heart rate never turned normal though, and we slowly and painfully tried to accept James' need for an artificial pacemaker. Dr. Chang explained, "Without James' temporary pacing wires, his heart rate would only be 40 to 50 beats per minute. This, of course, is dangerously low."

"Dr. Chang, how did this happen?" I asked. "I thought they repaired everything they needed to in that dreadfully long operation."

"Mrs. Mitchell, one of the risks involved in James' surgery was the possible destruction of his own electrical wiring," Dr. Chang began. "Had the surgical team stretched the surgery out to seven or eight hours, perhaps they could have had the time to save his internal pacemaker. But they weighed the risks and decided his body could not tolerate any additional time on the heart/lung machine. As they repaired the transposition and the other defects, his electrical circuit, the heart's own built-in pacemaker, was in the path and was damaged. It's the price he had to pay."

I wondered what else his heart would cost him. Pacemaker implantation was not considered major surgery and most people lived long, productive lives with them. But to me, the pacemaker represented trouble, a red flag highlighting his congenital heart disease.

The arrhythmia pace-maker specialist, Dr. Gamble, looked like an electrician with a pocket saver jammed with pens as he spoke in electrical terms of amps and volts. "The pacemaker device, referred to as a generator, is about the size of a cigarette lighter and emits electrical impulses that stimulate the heart to beat. The surgical team will tuck the device inside a pocket of fat in the lower part of his abdomen, to the left of his belly button. They will screw an electrical lead into the muscle of his heart and connect the other end of this wiring into the generator. The pacemaker will be monitored closely and when the battery life runs low, it will need to be replaced."

Here we go again. Just another round of technical, medical jargon to chew, gulp, and digest rapidly. The two hour pacemaker surgery proved more difficult to endure than the six hour open heart surgery seven days before. James had barely recovered before they were slicing into him again. This additional surgery was an indication life would never return to normal. Around every bend there would be another test, another procedure, and another hurdle to vault without question. I had surrendered to the first surgery. This new one, this new challenge, I resisted and with the struggle lost ground in acceptance and peace.

At times our life in the hospital seemed like a jumble of clothes, tossed about in a laundromat dryer. All the colors blurred in a swirl of confusion, with no order, no design or arrangement. Where were the iron and sturdy board to smooth out the details before being deluged with a new assignment? Would we never starch our life back into some crisp, manageable form or dimension? I yearned for the smell of the uncomplicated outdoors, clothes billowing in a soft, gentle breeze, strung together in a neat, orderly line.

But occasionally, as we tumbled about, the sweet scent of a country meadow entered. We slept in the parent's room, behind a thin hospital curtain, two cots squashed together. After our third night of restless sleep Bill received a phone call.

"Bill? John here."

"John? John who?"

"John Devine."

"Well, maybe you need to help me a bit. Tell me again why you're calling?"

"Friends of yours, Lou and Roland Henry, know our pastor. They attend our church whenever they're in Boston. Our pastor called. He explained your situation and asked us to call you. We have a home close to Children's. Why don't you move in with us for as long as you're at the hospital? It would be a thrill for us. Here's our address. Come around later this afternoon and check things out."

We did. Their large, comfortable house became a respite from the hospital and we knew God had provided us a haven in this foreign land. God continually reminded us that we were not abandoned. Sometimes a package from home arrived bursting with delicious, homemade goodies or a bulging envelope came stuffed with hundreds of notes from our Bible Study group. Once a beautiful spring bouquet arrived and stood as a symbol of hope on the receptionist's desk. Flowers were not allowed in the CICU, but we savored the beautiful arrangement every time we went in or out, feeling embraced by our friends who had thought to send them. Their note simply read, "Kneeling by the Throne on your behalf." Their succinct wording symbolized what hundreds were doing around the clock for our family.

We longed for our other three children intensely and after hearing their voices on the phone would limp around carrying an unbearable ache. When we discovered all three had the stomach flu and were vomiting in unison, I slumped between waves of depression and helplessness. We were in a difficult place, no end in sight, and no indication of when James would be well enough to travel home.

Home! Home was safe, comfortable and uncomplicated. Home was very far away. Homesickness engulfed me particularly at night, in the dark, in a strange bed, in a strange home, far, far away from anything familiar. Postpartum blues and breast infections did not help any.

Neither did the sight of so many parents in pain. I could barely manage our own misery, but when I peered into the haggard faces of parents staring helplessly at children they would never take home, the grief was staggering. One night after dinner we rode the elevator to the sixth floor with a bald-headed middle school girl. Her pale, thin face held eyes circled in black: a pitiful sight in plain view of everyone. Her parents' faces disclosed untold stories of mangled hopes and jumbled days. As we followed them off the elevator and down the long hallway, I felt physically ill for these perfect strangers. I desperately wanted to comfort them in some small way. Instead, I simply watched them walk away, trailing behind the gurney, as it disappeared into her room.

"Bill."

"Yes."

"If our own pain doesn't kill us, I think the pain I feel for others will."

"I know what you mean."

I knew he did. That night, while I waited for exhaustion to make way for sleep I still recalled the forlorn couple.

Lord, is this how you feel our pain? Because you suffered such physical torment, you actually feel our intense suffering. You understand exactly how we feel, don't you? Because you underwent such excruciating agony while you were on earth you have an incredible capacity to experience ours, don't you? God, tonight, I am, as always, totally helpless to make things better for James, and I physically ache for our other children. God, I long for all this dreadful stuff to go away quickly, but you want me to glimpse your depth of love for us, don't you? You fully understand everything we are going through. You can comprehend our loss, our frustration and our distress. You understand! You truly understand.

We might have been homesick but we were not forgotten as God continually sent messengers to remind us of this truth. Although we knew no one in Boston, nobody believed us because visitors showed up every day. Friends of our friends at home cheered us with gracious visits, kind gifts and meaningful conversations. Sometimes, perfect strangers were simply ministering angels God sent our way. One evening, when I was weepy and tired and longing for our children, one of our waiting room comrades invited us to join a group for dinner. We rode together in a taxi and found ourselves in a barbeque restaurant with a blazing fire and a boisterous atmosphere. I laughed through the entire meal and returned to the hospital feeling as if I had just taken a vacation.

Easter had always been vacation time and now it was approaching rapidly. But James' respiratory rate was also in rapid motion. His heart rate was good, the pacemaker was functioning fine, and he was nursing now and gaining weight. But his breathing was simply too fast. The days dragged and the nights seeped slowly by as we savored the dream of life returning to normal.

Then without warning, on the Saturday morning before Easter, 18 days after arriving in Boston, we heard the words, "You're free to go." While the nurses weighed his last diaper and disconnected one lingering IV line, we signed the release forms, packed our gear, listened to one more round of explanations on medications and follow-up procedures, then flew to the elevator, wings on our feet, James in our arms.

It was 2:30 in the afternoon on Saturday, April 10th, 1993, as I opened my Bible at the airport and picked up reading where I had left off. Psalm 91:14 was the Lord's farewell for this portion of our journey. "Because he loves me, says the Lord, I will rescue him. I will protect him for he acknowledges my name. He will call upon me and I will answer him. I will be with him in trouble. I will deliver him and honor him. With long life will I satisfy him and show him my salvation."

We had experienced every portion of that psalm. He had rescued us and answered when we called. He had been with us in trouble and had delivered us, honored us and satisfied our deepest longings by sparing James' life. Later, as we stepped off the plane into the brilliant light of three darling children, aunts, uncles, cousins and grandparents to escort us home triumphantly, our hearts truly knew deep satisfaction. We were free. Free at last. Free from hospital confines and fears of the unknown. Free from homesickness and James' sickness. Free to snuggle on the couch with our four precious children. Whatever lay ahead, we now knew we could deal with it.

Chapter 4

Unwelcome Intrusions

"If we obey God and trust in him, He will have compassion on us every day."

-James' Journal Entry, December 3, 2004

I 'M sorry to tell you this," Dr. Gamble explained on the phone, "but the generator is wearing down much quicker than we anticipated. It should be replaced promptly."

For eighteen months we had periodically relayed James' pacemaker numbers via a telephone hook-up directly from our home in Boca Raton to Dr. Gamble's office in Boston. The most recent transmission had prompted this unwelcome phone call. When he was ten days old, a week after the first open heart surgery, the pacemaker's leads had been placed on the outside of James' traumatized heart, forcing the pacer to drain energy more quickly. Another trip to Boston was inevitable.

The landscape of our lives had been littered with many unwelcome intrusions in the fall of 1994. My mother's sudden death in October had ripped our family to shreds, leaving us staggering from grief's cruel grip. She was only 56 years old when a massive stroke crept up and robbed us of her beautiful and extraordinary life. Two nights before the funeral, I suddenly awoke, my heart breaking into jagged pieces within my chest. As I sat on our couch in the darkness, enormous sadness washed over me in tidal waves and I sobbed aloud. I could not stop - I did not want to stop. My mother was no more. The invisible umbilical cord connecting us had been horrendously severed.

As my internal pressure mounted, I flicked on the lamp, reached for a pen and wrote furiously. I had prayed God would give me insights to share at her funeral and then, deep in the darkness, as the words tumbled out, I knew the Comforter had come.

THE STROKE COULD NOT ROB HER OF THAT

A massive stroke stalked Mummy eight years ago. It pinned her life to the mat and wrestled her very essence from her. The stroke demanded that everything in her life be confiscated, and it left her a prisoner in a chair on wheels. Like some smug sadist in a concentration camp, the stroke thought it had broken her and won.

But God said, "No. Pamela belongs to me. I will keep every promise I ever made to my beloved. I will never leave her or forsake her. She committed her life to me 12 years before. I will give her my grace to overcome. The stroke cannot rob her of that."

God said, "I will empower her husband Souhail with a limitless capacity to cherish his wife. I will pour out my strength and wisdom on him to enable him to selflessly love Pamela for me. Through him she will experience a depth of love only a privileged few ever know. He will be my hands, my feet, and my heart to care tenderly for my Pamela. The stroke cannot rob her of that."

Then God said, "I will wrap ten children round about her like a warm, woolen coat. They will be my arms to hug her. They will be my fire to warm her and keep out the cold. They will be my music, so she can hear my love songs written just for her. The stroke cannot rob her of that."

Then God said, "I will cause her family to prosper at her feet. I will give her 13 grandchildren to be my messengers of joy. They will deliver my love letters filled with hope, laughter and happiness.

They will sit in her lap for me. They will hug her tight for me. The stroke cannot rob her of that."

Then God said, "I will burn her name on the hearts of her faithful family and friends. They will love Pamela so much they will pray for her without ceasing. As they pray, my very angels will minister to Pamela, and I will give her courage to endure, strength to overcome, faith to believe and perseverance to withstand. The stroke cannot rob her of that."

But on Sunday last, the stroke demanded a re-match. It stood Goliath-like by her bed challenging her life again. This time, the stroke promised to steal even more from her. This time, it would imprison her in a coma and sentence her to a miserable existence.

But God said, "No! My daughter Pamela has suffered enough. I want her home. She belongs to me. It is time for me to carry her myself, to hold her and hug her in my very arms. It is time for me to cherish her to my very heart. I will not transfer her care to others anymore. Come, Pamela. Come home."

And the stroke could not rob her of that.

At the very same time we were dealing with Mummy's passing, we were flat broke, with nothing to spare and no pocket money anywhere in sight. Bill's real estate business was experiencing withdrawal pangs from the boisterous '80s, and we were deep into a recession. Dr. Gamble's call came at a time when we felt vulnerable emotionally, spiritually, financially, and physically.

But as we stood with the lining of our pockets flying bare in the breeze, God blew His resources into our life. An anonymous friend gave us two round-trip airline tickets to Boston, and my uncle's client, Barbra Ferdinando, a complete stranger to us, offered us her furnished apartment in Manchester, New Hampshire. We even received miraculous news by mail. The ambulance flight from West Palm Beach to Boston on the night James was born was billed to us at $10,000.00. The insurance company had refused to pay and the airline had forwarded us that staggering bill. We had no ability to pay, but God did. Without our knowledge, Bethesda Memorial Hospital, where James was born, had also billed the insurance company for the flight because on that first traumatic night when no insurance representative could be reached they agreed to cover the plane ride on our behalf. The insurance company paid the $10,000.00 when it came through from Bethesda!

Clearly, the God who had carried us through the first leg of our journey with James would do no less on this second lap around. He was challenging us to continue on the course He had laid out for us, confident of His provisions and His unwavering presence.

As an added bonus, God renewed us as we traveled to replace James' pacemaker. We spent the entire Friday at Boston Children's while they performed routine pre-op tests and consultations for the Monday pacemaker surgery. But the weekend was ours to enjoy, and Barbara sent a chauffeur to the hospital to drive us to Manchester. A scrumptiously stocked picnic basket greeted us in the back seat and our gracious hostess even had a stuffed toy tucked into the basket for James. Barbara met us at the door of a beautifully furnished apartment and greeted us as if we were her own children. She had packed the refrigerator with gourmet treats and provided us with a highchair, playpen, crib, car seat and a Mercedes Benz station wagon to explore Manchester.

We drank in the New England countryside, with its brilliantly dressed autumn maples reflected on the waters of Lake Winnipesaukee. We snapped pictures of James amidst piles of fallen leaves and marveled at God's grace that allowed us a feast when we couldn't afford a crumb. He enveloped us in extravagant love and poured healing into our wounded places.

He poured healing into James as well. The surgery went remarkably well and we returned home in two days with a brand new pacemaker tucked above James' heart. Surely all would be well for a long time. Surely God would not ask us to face any more hurdles soon.

CHAPTER 5

MAJOR MALFUNCTIONS

*I will try to always trust in the LORD, I will never be afraid or
terrified because I know that the LORD will never leave me."*
— *James' Journal Entry, March 4, 2005*

THE fool says in his heart there is no God; the greater fool
desires to be god and know what the future holds. To catch a
glimpse of 1997, to view the trio of traumatic events barreling
down the road towards us, would have been foolish, indeed.

In the first week of January, deep in the stillness of night, I studied
James as he slept and knew he was not well. He fought asthma now with
the use of a motorized nebulizer that shot steroids through a mist into
his nostrils. Three to four times a day I would strap an elasticized cup
over his nose and mouth while the machine pumped in the medication
to clear his lungs.

"James, I'm putting in your favorite video," I bribed.

"No, Mom. Not again. I don't want that stinky machine beside me
again."

"James, come on sweetie. The medicine will help you stop coughing.
Come sit here on Mommy's bed. Jacqui will sit beside you and you can
watch 'Animal Alphabet' together. When you're done, we'll do something
fun."

James was all about fun. We squeezed in life and all its wonder and excitement between trips to the cardiologist and the respiratory specialist. The cardiac medications, pacemaker monitoring, and asthma treatments were simply routine, and we wedged them into our regular family schedule beside basketball games, birthday parties, family bike rides and Sunday lunches with grandparents. James simply accepted the medical tests, the probing and the pills, along with trips to the beach and off-road adventures and frozen slushy drinks. He had brothers who wrestled him to the floor and taught him how to dribble a basketball, a sister who splashed with him in the pool and helped him ride a two-wheeler, and more than a dozen cousins living fifteen minutes away with whom to romp and run and discover the delights of childhood.

But when he couldn't breathe, we slowed down, strapped on the mask and waited for the medicines to work. His new cardiologist, Donna Rhoden, believed his breathing problems stemmed from the deformed mitral valve that had not functioned adequately from birth.

"Let's wait until he turns four and his heart is more capable of withstanding a cardiac catheterization," Dr. Rhoden recommended, after examining James in December. "This will determine the extent of the damage to his mitral valve, and we can decide then what our next step should be."

James' coughing and wheezing were intertwined within the fabric of our lives. We continued treating his asthmatic symptoms with visits to the respiratory specialist and round-the-clock nebulizer treatments, but somehow we grew accustomed to his ill health, routine doctor visits, and periodic trips to the emergency room when the asthma careened out of control.

But that January night was different. As I watched, James abruptly groaned, bolted forward, eyes wide, face chalky white, staring at me as if electrocuted. We flew to the emergency room.

"His pulse is 45," the nurse checking his vitals declared.

"That's not possible," Bill responded. "He has a pacemaker that's set at 100 beats per minute. Perhaps your monitor is broken."

The nurse sent us a puzzled look before placing his fingertips on

James' wrist. "I checked him the old fashioned way. My monitor is fine. His pulse is 45!"

Immediately the movement around James' bed intensified as the entire emergency room staff moved into response mode. The NICU physician ran tests and promptly reached his cardiologist and pacemaker technician. Within a short period they discovered defective pacemaker leads were the culprit. Depending on James' position or movement, the pacemaker leads would transmit the electrical stimuli to his heart or malfunction at will. Like a precarious roller coaster ride, James' heart would beat normally one moment and plummet to a dangerously low pulse rate the next. Somehow, during his routine pacemaker test the previous month, the leads were connected properly and tested perfectly.

In the early morning light Dr. Rhoden carefully prepared James for his ambulance escort to Jackson Memorial Hospital in Miami by implanting temporary pacing wires into his heart. With his favorite green pillow behind his head, we watched them load James into the ambulance, hopped in our car, and began the hour drive south.

About fifteen minutes into our trip Bill glanced into the rear view window and announced, "Here he comes."

The ambulance barreled from behind, sirens blaring, lights flashing, racing at 90 miles per hour. The driver's eyes were fixed steadily on the road, his hands firmly gripping the wheel. We felt anything but steady. How many times had we witnessed ambulances soaring by at neck-breaking speeds without any thought as to who was lying inside or where they were heading? This time, we observed our own son zoom past and realized afresh that we were incapable of controlling any part of our roller coaster romp.

James was placed under the care of Dr. Grace Wolfe, a distinguished pediatric cardiologist with an impressive history. She spoke kindly to James and in reassuring tones to us before directing her team to examine and evaluate James. But later, as they prepared him for surgery, Dr. Wolfe called me aside.

"Looking at the test results we have discovered a small mass that appears to be a blood clot inside James' heart. This adds quite a tricky element to the surgery. Placing a new pacemaker is fairly common place. But with the added twist of a blood clot with its capacity to dislodge at any moment and travel through the body causing irreparable damage, our risk factor just skyrocketed."

I had a sudden urge to throw up. Every muscle transformed into soft noodles and I gripped James' gurney tightly as they wheeled it toward the operating room. When the doors automatically shut behind them, I collapsed into the first chair. Bad news never grew easier to bear.

We sat listlessly in a dingy waiting room. Four rambunctious children took us hostage with noise which reverberated like pots banging right over my head. Our family arrived and sat vigil with us and, when the children turned up their volume, I handed my Bible to my brother Kary.

"Kary, would you mind reading aloud for us?" I closed my eyes in an attempt to block out the noise and focus on each phrase of the Psalms. Slowly, as each verse settled around us, as each familiar passage crowded in like old friends for support, the confusion and the clamor dissolved, leaving God's truth behind.

Isn't James His child? Doesn't James belong to Him? Isn't He fully capable of providing whatever James needs? Who's in control here, anyway? To be frightened, to allow the emergency to terrify, was to only pretend to be in control. Is it not the Father's full responsibility to fix our dreadful situation? Isn't God, Himself, right there in the operating room covering James with His own hand of protection? He is enough for darkness, enough for storms, enough for trembling hearts and pounding heads.

Half-way through the surgery my brother-in-law Rick walked into the stark waiting room, bag in hand. Without saying a word or asking any questions, he laid out a banquet on each of our laps. On other occasions, I have been treated to elaborate dinner parties and exotic restaurants, but none of them compared to this simple meal. Rick placed a Cuban sandwich and a bag of potato chips on my lap and propped an ice cold soda beside me. Once God had sent ravens to minister to Elijah; He was doing no less for us. Repeatedly, He used our loving family to minister to us. Once again, while we were bruised and battered on the side of the road, when everything seemed bleak and horrible, he sent his Samaritan to pour oil on our wounds. In that awkward waiting room, we experienced His royal treatment.

The pacemaker surgery was successful and the team decided to catheterize James and look closer at the clot. Dr. Wolfe emerged from the lab smiling. "We found no trace of the clot anywhere."

"Were you able to look at his mitral valve during the catheterization to see how badly damaged it is?" I asked.

"No, we never looked at it," she replied.

Why?

CHAPTER 6

JEREMIAH IN MIAMI

"God is a Just God and He knows what is best for His people."
-James' Journal Entry, April 6, 2006

L ITTLE boys in cowboy hats shouldn't ever have to throw up on their birthdays.

But James did. During his four-years-old celebration at a Playmobile Park, we slipped away twice as he struggled to breathe, walked across the parking lot, climbed into our van and hooked up the nebulizer for his asthma treatment. Afterward he stuck his head out the car door, threw up, replaced his cowboy hat, and sauntered back inside. John Wayne could have taken lessons.

The next day I consulted with Dr. Rhoden, and she scheduled a heart catheterization at Miami Children's Hospital for the morning of June 24, 1997. Dr. Anthony Chang, the first cardiologist to talk with Bill that night in Boston, had recently taken a position there.

But as June 24th approached, I sank beneath the sickening load, collapsing under the weight of placing James in another hospital. I dreaded taking our gentle, golden haired boy back to further struggling and suffering and the unknown. The heaviness turned to gloom and I slumped on the sofa, Bible open on my lap. I begged, pleaded, and prayed.

"God, I can't go this way again. Don't ask me to go down this road again. It's too dark. It's a long, frightful tunnel. Don't ask me to go there, Father. I can't do it again."

As my internal struggle intensified, I forced myself to read the Scriptures. The words saturated the fog and compelled me to linger. Listless, I hid for a while in the unlikely book of Jeremiah where God had given the Israelites a message of hope thousands of years before. In His gracious way, he passed the message along to me. The Israelites were not to fear captivity in Babylon; I was not to fear going to Miami. God reminded the Israelites that He would bless them in this foreign land far more than he would provide for them in Israel. God would bless us even in an undesirable cardiac unit.

As I waited before Him, curled on that couch, the Father gently whispered to my heart,

> *Daughter of mine. I know you would be willing to face any mission field I sent you to. If I asked you to go to the ends of the world, I know you would eagerly pack your bags and embrace the adventure. Daughter, think of Miami in this way: I am asking you to go as my emissary to that hospital, to that place that seems so frightening now. Remember, I am with you always. Do this for me.*

So I packed our bags for the hospital because He had lovingly brought me to a place of surrender. In yielding to His way, He gave me a sweet peace that nothing could unpack.

We arose early that Tuesday morning, June 24th, piled into the car and eased onto the highway. James was half-asleep in his car seat until I turned around and pointed to the brilliant rainbow with its entire arch painted across the full length of the morning sky. Like a gigantic banner, it waved God's faithfulness directly in our face.

"James, do you see that big rainbow?"

"Yeah."

"God put it there just for us. He wants us to know He is going to take care of you. It's a picture of a promise."

The day lengthened into a grueling march as James complained irritably because he could not eat or drink anything. When the technician attempted to draw blood, he expressed his disapproval loudly.

Dr. Zann, who would perform the heart catheterization, explained, "We'll do the procedure in the cath lab. I will insert the probe through the vein in his groin and then I'll be able to read his pressures and clearly see what condition the chambers and valves are in presently. Hopefully, we can buy some time, send you home and have James come back in a few months for more tests. The older he is for his next surgery, the better, of course."

"How long is this procedure?"

"An hour, or so. I'll come out and talk with you as soon as I can." He turned and we watched his white coat retreat. We fidgeted for that hour and instantly sprang from our plastic chairs when Dr. Zann returned.

"I'm going to recommend that you admit James immediately."

His words slammed into our chests like a truckload of bricks.

"His mitral valve must be replaced and his heart is significantly enlarged – it's about the size of an adult's. It's not advisable to wait."

"You mean, right now! Today! How soon will you do the surgery?" I asked.

"I won't," Dr. Zann replied. "Dr. Redmond Burke will probably be the surgeon. He'll answer all your questions. Let's get James admitted. Let's get him well."

As Dr. Rhoden suspected, all James' respiratory problems had been caused by regurgitation from the mitral valve. Because of its abnormal function, this valve that lies between the left atrium and the left ventricle did not close sufficiently after the blood surged through. Instead, the blood regurgitated backward causing fluid to lodge in the pulmonary areas and create his "cardiac asthma" condition. With an artificial mitral valve, all his pulmonary problems would be solved as well.

In a short while we were admitted to the Pediatric CICU with Dr. Chang clarifying the prognosis. "James will be in the CICU for about five days. We'll treat him with potent doses of cardiac medications to strengthen his heart adequately to undergo surgery. Dr. Burke will meet with you and go over all the particulars of the surgery. He's the best there is."

James looked frail in the large hospital bed, but he was thrilled when they finally allowed him to sip a soda. He was hooked to monitors that gauged his blood pressure, heart rate, respiratory rate and oxygen level, but he was oblivious to all the monitors and screens encircling his cubicle. He gave his full attention to the TV screen in front of his bed and the icy cold Sprite in his hand.

When he finally fell asleep, Bill and I found the linens and fixed our cots in the parent lounge. We talked to the children at home, trying to reassure them that it would not be too long until we returned.

In the stillness of the early morning, before the day galloped into full swing, I sat beside James' bed and wrote him a letter.

June 25, 1997

Dear James,

As I write this, you lie asleep before me in a cubicle bed in an Intensive Care Room at Miami Children's Hospital. We packed our bags, you and me, because it was summer, and summer is a time for getting away and seeing new places and allowing the breeze to blow stuffy cobwebs out of our brains.

But, instead, we had to take a trip here for them to blow more serious stuff out of your lungs and your heart. There will be time, in other June hours, to go for picnics and build castles by the shore and bridges to far off lands. For now, you must feed on oxygen piped in your nose and medicines pumped in your heart.

I want you to know how God came with us - with you and Daddy and me-on all the adventures He has asked us to travel. How God came near and whispered comfort in our ears and cheer into our grieved spirits and hope when all was gone. God has never once, never for a moment of time, abandoned us on the way. He will never abandon you.

Perhaps when you read these words you will be older and wiser but still faced with struggle. I do not know what life will hold for you, my darling. I do not know how many more surgeries you must face, brave and strong. But I know this – He never failed you when your shoots were tender, when your hair was light sunshine splashing on your face, when scars first marked your chest and you were forced to learn of pain and shots and tubes and fears. He did not let you down then; He will hold you fast now.

I have no answers to the why of all of this. Why the need for five surgeries with scars and pumps of artificial form to nudge your own chambers to move and throb. I have no answers as to why He chose to allow you to know pain and difference and struggle in the simple act of breathing. Why He chose to keep His hands by His side when your heart was being formed. Why He chose to turn His head away when deep within my womb you lay, not as you should have been. Why now He chooses not to heal your mitral valve with the lightest touch of his fingertips.

No, my son, he has a greater plan for you – he has chosen to use your life for His purposes, His ways. Far beyond my comprehension, He knows all and does all well. He knows the why, and I must rest my why on Him. I want you always to rest yours there as well. He is, after all, our Infinite caregiver- lover of my soul and yours. I pray He will give you the grace you will need all your life to deal with what He asks of you.

June 26, 1997/10:00 a.m.

Dear James,

You are asleep again, looking like a tiny angel with golden hair. They've moved your surgery closer by five days and scheduled it for today. Now is the calm before the storm.

We played this morning, and I enjoyed your laughter, loved teasing with you. Then your body slumped and you laid your head against your green pillow with no more desire or energy left in you. This has been your pattern for a while now, up then down, active then suddenly weary and worn.

Like a swift kick in my gut, I reeled back from the news last evening as the doctors detailed your new status. More days of tune-up in the ICU would not benefit you as they first thought. It is wiser, they believe, to do the surgery promptly. Your heart is huge, the size of an adult's, and you need an artificial mitral valve. The surgeon will enter your sweet body from the side, in between your rib cage. Dr. Burke has perfected this method of surgery that avoids cutting through your sternum and peeling back the scar tissue from your previous operation.

The surgery will be five hours long. They will replace your old valve, a worn and weary soldier that has kept vigil for you these past four years of life, and put in a metal valve, covered with Teflon. We will bring in a new comrade, strong, solid, artificial, to open and close the door to the chambers of your heart.

I stand by your bed now and feel the urge to slip off my shoes. The place where I stand is Holy ground; God is at His work. It is a sacred place where God is allowing us to suffer and know a generous serving of pain. It is a privilege to be a part of acute, intense, unrelenting pain. I feel layers of myself peeling off, like a bruised onion. Which dragon-skinned layer is He peeling away now? I desperately want the Lord to be seen in me and I know He will slice away all the parts that do not resemble Him.

I have read much Scripture sitting beside your bed. I know I am naked and cold and that He will dress me in His warmth. I am a shivering, hungry waif who begs for crumbs; He supplies a feast for me in His word and encircles me with His royalty.

✳   ✳   ✳

After completing the letter I continued reading in Psalm 105:1-5 and realized the precise response God desired was mapped out in these few lines. Right there in black and white for me to clearly identify and engraft into my heart God was telling me I should give Him thanks, call out to His name, and make known among the nations what He has done for us. As I studied those verses He reminded me to sing praises to Him, to tell others of His wonderful acts and to make sure I brought glory to His name. I was to seek the Lord with all my heart, rejoice, look to the Lord for strength, seek God's face all the time and remember the wonders He has done for us.

I continued to Psalm 108: "My heart is steadfast, O God; I will sing and make music with all my soul." What an odd thought! I was being asked to make music with all my soul. *Lord, help my soul to be so in tune with you that it will produce beautiful music to your ears.*

I had no idea when God led me to Psalm 105 that morning how desperately I would need a plan of action for the evening ahead.

CHAPTER 7

A SOLDIER'S SONG

I want to look at God and always seek His face even in hard times."

— James' Journal Entry, April 22, 2005

JAMES was restless, irritable and hungry all afternoon. He could not eat or drink before the operation, and he was not one bit pleased.

"James, you know, they don't let soldiers have any food or drink when they're going on a special assignment," I carefully explained, bending over his bed. "They have to hide out in caves or jump out of planes for secret assignments and they can't eat either. You have to be a brave soldier too. They'll let you eat soon. But for now, you have to be a very brave soldier."

His large brown eyes stared back at me. His voice was hoarse, his lips cracked and dry. "Mom, I don't even want to be a soldier."

I couldn't blame him. I didn't want him to be a soldier, either.

A short while later, we escorted our trooper to the operating room and smiled at his silly reactions to the intravenous sedative. They pushed his gurney through the large doors as he waved a courageous farewell. Perhaps someday I would grow up to be as brave as our little boy.

Our family members encircled the spacious waiting area like

warriors intent on protecting us. We prayed aloud, read the Bible aloud, then talked quietly - waiting, wondering, hoping. The night before, Dr. Burke had explained the surgery as being fairly routine, one in which he did not anticipate any complications.

Joanne, the nurse practitioner, was the liaison between the surgical team and our family, and she interrupted our circle periodically to bring updates from the operating room. With her calm tone and carefully chosen words, Joanne informed us when James was totally under anesthesia, when they had chilled his body to the required low temperature, and when he was fully dependant on the heart-lung machine.

One hour later she returned to relay that Dr. Burke had made the incision through James' right ribcage, and on her next visit we learned the team had removed the dilapidated mitral valve and replaced it with the artificial one. When Joanne reported that Dr. Burke was now in the process of closing James' incision, the noise level instantly increased and the collective emotional pressure in the room fell into a normal range. Someone broke out the snacks and we munched to pass the time until Joanne's next positive update.

An hour passed. Joanne would be returning soon. Thirty more minutes slowly seeped away. Perhaps she was tied up with another patient. She should be coming soon now. Our eyes stayed riveted on our watches; our heart rates increased. The door cracked and we riveted our eyes on Dr. Chang, standing there in surgical garbs, paper covered shoes. He looked directly at us and motioned with his finger. "Only the parents, please."

He didn't speak another word while we followed him down the corridor, into the CICU, desperate for his report. He fumbled around, opening and shutting doors in an attempt to locate an empty consultation area. Finally, he simply pulled up three chairs to one side of a vacant desk and motioned for us to sit down.

"We cannot get James off the heart-lung machine." He spoke in slow, deliberate phrases. "His heart will not start on its own."

The floor opened beneath me. My lungs tightened, every breath frozen inside. What was he saying? Why couldn't I understand? His face was close to mine but it seemed his voice came from a great distance away.

His voice continued, "We have to buy some time, to give James' left ventricle time to regroup. We must connect him to a Left Ventricle Assist Device, which will allow his own left ventricle to rest as the machine does all the pumping and circulating for his heart."

I could hardly understand his explanations. The foreign terms slammed into my mind like any alien spaceship intent on destruction. I forced myself to look at his lips and heard, "There are only two of these machines available in our entire hospital. Most hospitals don't even have this complex equipment for their pediatric patients. We perfected this machine here at Children's. One of them is already being used and we're connecting James to the other."

"Dr. Chang, what happened?" Bill demanded.

"When we replaced James' valve with a strong, artificial one, the procedure was successful. But the muscles of his heart were just too flabby. They were too weak to adapt to a working valve with the full force of the blood supply surging through the chambers."

For James' entire life his mitral valve had been inadequate for the blood supply. Because they never worked correctly, the muscles in the left ventricle were soft and flabby. They just could not take the full force of the blood supply pumping through."

"Dr. Chang," I cried aloud, "we waited too long! We took too long to do the surgery! Why, why didn't we do the surgery before when his heart was stronger?" I pounded his leg with my palm as I spoke.

"How long can he be connected to this machine?" Bill questioned him, his eyes red and his voice tight.

"Well, we'll try to wean him off of it as soon as possible. Give us time. You'll be able to see him in a while."

"Suppose it doesn't work." Bill spoke with his eyes to the floor.

"We have options," Dr. Chang replied. "We'll talk about our options later."

A vacuum cleaner had just been jabbed into our bellies and the contents sprayed back in our faces. "Can we have some time alone?" asked Bill, his voice trembling and low.

Dr. Chang beckoned Joanne who had been standing quietly to one side. She guided us to a vacant CICU cubicle and closed the curtain.

We wept.

Bill slumped to the tiled floor after pulling a rocking chair towards me. A short distance away, our little boy was dying, his heart failing, and we were helpless.

"God," I cried aloud. "Help us! Do for us what we can't do."

Remember the wonders He has done, sing praises to His name. Psalm 105 replayed in my head. *Not now! Not here in the middle of this mess.* Yes, right now, especially right now, in the middle of this mess. Yes, yes, I must sing praises. God had given me an outline earlier today. He had known what was to come; He had prepared me for this.

I touched Bill's shoulder and quietly, ever so quietly, sang. "I must tell Jesus all of my troubles. I cannot bear this burden alone. I must tell Jesus; I must tell Jesus. Jesus will save me; Jesus alone."

I repeated the chorus again. Joni Erickson Tada had shared that song on her radio program days before we came to Miami. The interviewer had asked how Joni comforted those who were grieving. What did she say to those in great pain? Joni replied that often words were inadequate; sometimes she simply sang. Now, her haunting melody, the simple truth, spilled from me as well.

I heard Bill pray, "Father. You have given James to us as a gift. He has been one of the sweetest joys of our life. Father, if it is your will for us to lose him, we know you do all things well. We give him back to you. We offer him back to you. Do what you know to be best."

We sat for a long time, unable to return to the waiting room. It seemed miles away. What would we say? How could we ever explain what had happened? But I was determined our family would hear the news from us, and we scraped ourselves off the floor, walked down the hall, opened the waiting room door and faced a room of anxious faces.

"They can't get James off the heart-lung machine," I began. "His heart can't restart. The left ventricle has given out."

It was Mom's soft crying that pierced me first as we choked out the rest of the horrible news. I read my own horror reflected on my sisters' faces. Our son Billy was seated on the floor, and I slid down beside him, held him close, needing to feel his flesh against mine. We prayed; a circle of grieving hearts. Once again I asked Kary to read the Bible and once again the Great Shepherd used His Word to walk us through the valley of the shadow of death. As I sat on the hard floor I sensed the presence of the Lord and my heart responded in song.

"I cast all my cares upon you," I sang quietly, my eyes tightly closed. "I lay all of my burdens down at your feet. And anytime I don't know what to do, I will cast all of my cares upon you."

* * *

Perhaps if he had stepped on a land mine the damage would have been less severe. When we were allowed to see him, his head was propped awkwardly to one side, to facilitate the prongs protruding from the incisions in his neck and rib cage. Dry, cracked lips and sunken eyelids rimmed in black highlighted his pathetic face. Two gigantic, transparent hoses pulsing with his blood were connected to the prongs. They swirled across his body and coiled snake-like across every inch of the sheets. The Left Ventricle Assist Device (LVAD) positioned at the bottom of his bed was constantly monitored by a technician who orchestrated the machine as it rerouted James' entire blood supply away from his damaged left ventricle.

In order for this bypass machine to function, the nurses administered huge doses of the blood thinner Coumadin to enable James' blood to maneuver through the machine and adjoining tubes. But the effect was gruesome. The thinned blood trickled like water from a leaky faucet; a bright, red flag warning of impending danger. I touched his blood-matted hair and gazed at his pitiful form as the nurse attempted to sop the blood with gauze pads. James lay inches from death and looked it, stretched out thin and lifeless in his drug induced coma.

We dozed, rose early, and staggered out wearily to stand guard at James' side. His cubicle was jammed with the new life-saving equipment and we were only allowed in for brief periods at a time. Very little had changed; the nurses moved incessantly, injecting great quantities of medications, and the technician rarely took a break from piloting the bypass machine. It was only Friday, June 27th, but surely a lifetime had passed since we had entered the hospital. After a while, I slipped onto a stool in a corner of the ICU cubicle and opened my Bible. Romans 8:6 read, "…but the mind controlled by the Spirit is life and peace." I prayed that His divine Spirit would be in complete control of us, of James, of every overwhelming scenario being played out before our eyes.

Bill's Bible lesson the week before had been in I Peter, Chapter 5, but verse 10 made far greater sense to me now as I sat looking at James connected to that machine. "And the God of all grace, who called you to his eternal glory in Christ, after you have suffered a little while, will himself restore you and make you strong, firm and steadfast. To him be the power for ever and ever. Amen."

Oh, Father, won't you restore James. Won't you make him strong, firm and steadfast? Father, help us as you call us to suffer a 'little while'. We can only do this if we have your power.

When the commotion began increasing around James, I retreated to the waiting room. No human being could comfort us; no one could make our nightmare vanish. We were languishing in desperation on a deserted island with God as our only hope of rescue. I needed His voice, His arms, and His assuring presence. I curled myself in the plastic chair and turned again to I Peter.

"In this you greatly rejoice, though now for a little while you may have had to suffer grief in all kinds of trials. These have come so that your faith - of greater worth than gold, which perishes even though refined by fire - may be proved genuine, and may result in praise, glory and honor when Jesus Christ is revealed" (I Peter 1:6-7).

Father, if Jesus Christ is honored and given glory through our trial, He is revealed. He is seen in us in the middle of this trial. Lord, that is what you want, isn't it? You want to be seen in us, right here, right now. Make it so, Lord. Make it so.

I could read without interruptions in the isolated room and I flipped over to the Book of James. As I read the first few verses of Chapter 1, God began answering many of my troublesome questions. Why was James going through this again? How was I to consider this part of our life a joy? If I focused on James' wounded, bleeding body, I lost all perspective. But if I forced myself to focus on what God was doing, then, only then, could I begin to understand and trust.

He was asking me to persevere. I must learn to battle like a soldier and not despair. God was about maturing me, completing me, filling in all the places I lacked. I must consider our crises an opportunity to experience God's joy because He was completing the incomplete, the immature parts of me.

But I was weak, incomplete, and I fell apart with the next batch of medical updates. The doctors began weaning James off the LVAD, slowly, carefully, methodically. While the machine allowed his left ventricle to rest, it also physically assaulted his heart. In a very real sense, James was connected to a time bomb waiting to detonate, and his own left ventricle must be forced to take back its assigned responsibility.

But the plan backfired. As his heart began to respond and take over a greater percentage of the workload, the left ventricle suddenly, violently collapsed. I glimpsed a herd of white coats converging on James' cubicle and I cowered in the waiting room. It was late afternoon in the outside world, but midnight on that floor.

I curled my legs tightly underneath me as I felt frost beneath my skin. I wrapped myself in a white hospital blanket, but it brought no relief. I could not walk to the CICU; I dared not look at James. I simply could not face seeing him so close to death.

"God, I cannot do this," I moaned out loud, my eyes tightly shut and our family sitting helplessly around me. "God, if you want to take James home, if you think it would be best for him, God, I release him to you. I know you know what is best. But God, you have to help me here. I'm drowning in this thing. Give me the grace to handle what you are asking of me. Give me the grace to let him go. God, oh, God, help us. Help us, God. Help us."

Darkness filled the room and family members trickled out to check on James. Bill stayed in the CICU, but I never left the waiting room. I felt frozen, and I opened the cot and tried to sleep. Maybe if I slept, this would go away. Maybe when I awoke I would be able to handle this.

But sleep would not come to soothe or steal me away. Bill dragged himself into the room, his eyes bloodshot, his shoulders drooping, and lay on the cot beside me. He looked too exhausted to make conversation, and I could not handle knowing there had been no improvement. If I could just thaw out and stand up and go to James. If I could only stop feeling so very cold!

The darkness in the room pressed against my chest; I was suffocating. Dread seeped into every cell and fear clawed its way into every nerve. If only someone would come and make this go away. If only someone was still here to tell me what was happening.

I yearned to rise up and check on James. What time was it now? It was darker than it had ever been. I finally struggled up from the cot, wrapped the blankets around my shoulders and paced back and forth in front of my bed. If only I could open the door and walk down the hall to the ICU. Instead, I turned and crawled back under the covers and curled my legs tightly beneath me.

Then the door cracked and in the sliver of light from the hall I saw my father's figure. He was still there; he had not left. My two sisters-in-law crept quietly into the room, fearful of waking us.

"I thought you were all gone," I said, sitting up quickly, relief washing over me.

"No, Lizzie. We've been here. We haven't left." Haifa bent forward and held me as if I were a small child.

"How's James?" I asked.

"He's holding on. He's okay."

I glanced at my father's face. "Dad, how's James?"

"Sweetheart, don't be afraid," his calm voice reassured me. "Don't let your heart be troubled. James is going to be fine. Didn't I tell you already? God gave me a promise, and I know James is going to come through this. I am not afraid for James. I don't want you to be either. Try to sleep now, honey. It's going to be okay."

Kary and Haifa drove Dad home but Paul and Jill remained in the room, keeping vigil over James, over us. "Jill," I whispered, trying not to wake Bill. "I'm so afraid."

She slipped over and sat on the cot. "Elizabeth, God is not asking you to watch James die. James is not dying now. If God calls you to that place, He will give you the grace you need for that. You think James is dying, but you have jumped ahead of God. You have always told me that He has always given you peace to handle whatever He has asked you to go through. He is not asking you to give James up yet. Satan is trying to cripple you, to make you lose focus. This fear is not from God."

I listened intently to her lecture, soaking up her counsel. She was right. I had allowed my own fears to paralyze me. I had given up hope that God could help us. That was it! I had simply lost hope. I had forgotten who God was and what He could do.

Lord, would you give me a verse to focus on to block out this cold, dark fear? Would you fill up my entire mind with your word so there is no room left for fear? Would you give me a picture of yourself as a shield against my dreadful, anxious thoughts? I know Satan is trying to destroy us. This fear is so consuming, I know it comes from him. You are not the author of confusion, and I have been frightfully confused. Don't allow him to destroy us, Father.

I lay still, closed my eyes to all the blackness around me, and waited. Moments passed and a peaceful picture posed itself in my mind. A small boat battled a ferocious storm. I sat on a wooden bench in the stern of the boat and James stood directly in front of me with his arms wrapped around the legs of a tall man. I could not see the gentleman's face, but I could clearly distinguish that he had one hand on James' back and the other steering the boat. I distinctly saw James as healthy, strong and vibrant even while the waves crashed around the boat. The serene image lingered, filling every crevice of my mind. I did not need to carry James. Christ would. I was incapable of shouldering this acute burden, but I wasn't being asked to. My job was to stay in the boat in the storm until we reached the other side. Just stay in the boat. Rest and wait. God was at the helm and would navigate through this storm.

My mind remained framed by this beautiful picture and then, surprisingly, I recalled the story in the Gospel of Mark that I had read earlier in the week. The disciples were also in a boat in a storm, straining against the waves, struggling to survive. As Christ approached them, they were terrified at his presence. I remember being struck by the phrase He spoke to them: "Take courage. It is I. Do not be afraid" (Mark 6:50). He climbed into the boat and the storm disappeared. Now as we were besieged by our own version of a catastrophic storm, the Lord gave me a picture directly connected to the verse. The verse took up residence in my mind: "Take courage, Elizabeth. It is I. Do not be afraid. It is I. It is I. Trust me. Take courage from me. Do not be afraid. Allow me to take you through the storm."

Like a gigantic broom sweeping away hideous cobwebs, the verse and the picture it had created eased away my anxious thoughts. I thawed, and, finally, I slept.

In the light of morning, I could face James once more. I crept into his room, gazed at his beautiful form, and did not focus on all the hideous mess around him. I pulled out my Bible again and continued in the book of James. I prayed verse five back to God. *Father, you know we lack wisdom. The doctors do, too. Give us all wisdom from your mind, your heart.*

In the afternoon the surgeons made a decision to re-open James' incision in his ICU cubicle because he was too unstable to be transported to the operating room. They drew the curtains shut; we drew our circle of family to prayer.

Hours later, Dr. Jacobs emerged triumphantly. With a beaming smile he explained, "We discovered that blood had seeped out of the incisions, forming clots that filled the cavity around his heart. Because his blood had been significantly thinned for the LVAD, vast amounts had drained out in a short period of time. The clots left the heart little room to work efficiently. As we evacuated around the heart and removed the clots, I literally saw the heart begin to beat stronger right before my eyes. It was amazing!"

We soared. Once again, God had given the surgeons the wisdom to save James' life.

When laughter filled the CICU cubicle later that evening, God himself must have smiled. Two friends, Debbie and Kris, chose to spend the night with me so Bill could be with the kids at home. Kris and her husband Dan had been on vacation with their family when James' heart collapsed. We had attempted to reach them without success but as soon as they discovered we needed them, they drove through the night to be at our side.

The nurse asked us to massage lotion on James' feet and hands to help reduce his fever. His warm skin felt tight and dry and we willing obliged, grateful to be assigned a task that could possibly benefit James. As we worked, Kris sang a beautiful praise song in her deep alto voice, and Debbie and I joined in. One song led to many more, and we worshipped our Lord right there to the accompanying rhythm of the LVAD. Then, because it grew late and we grew tired, we giggled and one giggle led to many more. The night before I never imagined I would ever laugh again. Only God could fill us with His hope as we enjoyed the high privilege of ministering to James. When we finally gained control, stopped singing and put down the lotion, we glanced at the monitors. His fever had dropped dramatically.

Before we left for bed, I attempted to wipe away some of the blood matted into his hair. His head was still cocked awkwardly to one side, and I ran my hand beneath his neck, acutely aware of his frailty. Our tiny warrior had been asked to battle foes on the frontline. Bravely, he held on. Beating all the odds, he held on. Sliced by swords, sharp and menacing, he held on. I held him now. God held us both.

Before drifting off to sleep, I turned to 2 Corinthians 4:16 and He reminded me, "…therefore, we do not lose heart." I read further, but that one phrase replayed itself. I no longer pleaded for God to spare James' life. Instead, I simply praised him for enabling us not to lose heart.

I awoke Sunday morning with fresh hope surging through me. It was 6:30 and in the stillness on the floor, before doctor's rounds, phone calls or visitors began, I looked at Luke, Chapter 1. Mary's praise for her Lord reflected exactly how I felt. "And Mary said, 'My soul glorifies the Lord and my spirit rejoices in God my Savior, for He has been mindful of the humble state of His servant. From now on all generations will call me blessed, for the Mighty One has done great things for me – holy is his name. His Mercy extends to those who fear Him, from generation to generation. He has performed mighty deeds with His arm.'"

I continued reading in Luke and came across Jesus healing the leper, the paralytic and the centurion's servant. I reviewed these familiar, Sunday School felt-board stories, but saw Christ's compassionate love as if for the first time. As I lingered, looking at the miracles He performed with such ease, I sought for Him to do the same for James. There, in that sterile, hospital room, I prayed earnestly for His miraculous touch to cover James. Christ was the same yesterday, today and forever. I called out to the Great Physician, knowing His will was perfect, His ways beyond understanding. I wanted Him to heal James. I knew He would do what was best.

In so many ways He had already made Himself known to us. Throughout the entire ordeal, our family and our church family had touched us with His gentleness, whether they brought food, came to cheer us on, cared for the other children or took our laundry home. Each act of kindness brought brilliant light into our dreary days. Every familiar face, delicious meal, and thoughtful card was a continual reminder that God was keenly aware of our needs and fully capable of meeting every one.

Late Sunday night, after the last visitor had returned home and we finally unfurled our cots, James had been weaned 90% off the machine. The LVAD was now only pumping for James 10% of the time. Our sparsely decorated sleeping quarters suddenly seemed luxuriant.

Monday, June 30, 1997

Dear James,

Just as Hannah prayed and pleaded for a son while she was in the temple, I prayed and pleaded for your life early Saturday morning. Following her example, I surrendered your life completely to the Lord for Him to use for His service. I want to record this because I never want to forget what God did for us.

Son of My Womb

Son of my womb, lamb of my life
Gentlest joy are you.
Sweet precious spirit, laughter and love
Lamb of my life are you.
We gave you to Jesus,
Again,
Yielded your life to the throne,
In anguish and pain, again and again,
We yielded your life to the throne.
Lamb of my life, I laid you
Whisper of wonder, so fair
In tender mercy, he listened
He heard every word, every prayer.
Now as I wait, I wonder
I ponder His truths and sing
Your ways are higher than mine,
Lord,
Your way is everything.

It was 7:30 Monday evening when Dr. Jacobs, the two technicians, George and Todd, and three OR attendants pushed James' bed out of the CICU. We walked beside James to the operating room where they would attempt to disconnect James completely from the LVAD.

Dr. Jacob looked at us confidently and declared, "It's going to be a great night!"

He was right. Two hours later he and Dr. Burke returned looking like knights dressed in green surgical armor who had just slain a dreadful dragon. "He did great! James' heart is beating completely on its own!"

Twenty-five people rocked the waiting room with cheers and applauded the startled physicians. When they left, we held hands, twenty-five weaklings suddenly made strong, and praised our Father in heaven, who chose to extend mercy to a handful of His children. We laughed, embraced and pulled out cell phones to send the miraculous news to others. Our exuberance filled the room, broke through the doorway and spilled all over that cardiac floor.

Suddenly, someone shouted, "They're bringing James back from the OR."

"Quick, quick, here he comes!"

We rushed to the doorway and glimpsed his pale body freed of prongs and hoses and machines being pushed past us back to the CICU. He simply looked asleep; the warrior waiting to be awoken.

It was past midnight when I watched his night nurse, Betty, give him a bath. "We're weaning him off all the meds that kept him in a coma. He should be alert by morning," she explained without looking up from her task. As Betty washed his hair it struck me as odd; it was the only normal thing done to him since we entered this place.

After a short nap I returned to the CICU, too elated to sleep. James was off that dreadful machine and the reports had all been positive. I poked my head in. "How's he doing, Betty?"

She responded cautiously, without her usual quick humor. "I'm getting some movement on his right side, but nothing on his left."

"What do you mean?" My voice came out tight.

"Well, he could have suffered a stroke. It's one of the side-effects of the assist device. He was on all that Coumadin, the blood thinner, for the LVAD. Blood that thinned out could have created problems in his brain as well."

"Betty, are you sure?"

"Let's not worry just yet. Let's wait and see. We'll know more in the morning."

In the morning we did know more, more than we ever wanted to know. It required two hours and two transport paramedics to prepare him to go downstairs for a CAT scan, shift him onto a gurney and monitor his respirator and IV lines on the way to the lab. How unfair that God would not even allow us one day to bask in our victory before He forced us to face another gigantic, insurmountable hurdle.

We sat limply outside the CAT lab with the cement truck back on our chests, Kathy and Kary riding side-saddle once again. The stroke diagnosis had reopened all the painful memories of our mother's suffering and death.

We were distracted by a young boy, perhaps seven or eight years old, in a wheelchair, giggling with his mother. Fish-like eyes bulged from a severely deformed face which had apparently undergone multiple reconstructive and plastic surgeries. It was obvious he had many more surgeries to face. But he was smiling and playing games with his mother, oblivious to our presence in the corridor.

Dr. Chang strode down the hall and slipped quickly into the CAT lab. He re-emerged minutes later. "James has suffered a stroke on the right side of his brain. We don't know yet how much of the left side of his body will be affected. I've called in a neurologist to assess him."

"Oh, no, God! Not this too," slipped out of my lips.

Dr. Chang left us to grapple with this monster. I wanted to throw myself on the carpet, kick and scream, but I couldn't. Right in front of me sat the young boy with his mother. God had posted a brilliant neon sign in plain view. *Don't you dare feel sorry for yourself or for James. Look at what others endure. Stop complaining. Focus on all you have to be thankful for.*

I quit whining fast.

Chapter 8

Unending Mercy, Grateful Hearts

"I can be thankful to the LORD for all the good things He has blessed me with because I know that His love will always flow on me."

— *James' Journal Entry, May 4, 2006*

OBSERVING the neurologist as he methodically evaluated James' deficiencies from the stroke proved excruciating. James cringed with each probe and prod; I drooped.

But Dr. Chang stayed to chat on his evening rounds and lingered in the room long enough to bring hope. "Strokes in children are unlike adults because children can recover almost all of their faculties in a fairly short period of time. Of course, James will need extensive physical and occupational therapy; we want to be aggressive with his treatment. I'm having them come two to three times a day. The quicker we begin this process, the greater are James' chances of recovery."

But therapy was plain, hard work and the warrior was plum tuckered out. We persevered; relentless, unswerving, diligent. Keep going now, this is no time to falter. But at the outset of our second week in Miami, when weariness knocked at the door, we answered. God understood; He knew precisely what we could endure, heard the cry of our strength-sapped spirits and replied with His Spirit of gratefulness. I awoke early that morning overcome with delight to the Lord for a good night of sleep, for James' slow improvements, for allowing us to be in a wonderful hospital, for the dedicated, caring staff, for another day to care for James. Before my feet even touched the tiled floor I savored the delightful thought that I had not used up one bit of God's mercy or His grace. Enough was available for the day; I hadn't spent it all yesterday. No matter how many times I had needed His help and called out to Him and depended on Him, I hadn't used up all His resources because He had a limitless supply. He would carry us through again, and again, and still yet again. His mercies would never run out. He was always enough, always more than enough.

As I read the Scriptures, the comforting message in 2 Corinthians 1:8-11 compelled me to copy them in oversized letters in my journal. I placed the open notebook at the bottom of James' bed and read the enlarged words repeatedly throughout the day.

"We were under great pressure, far beyond our ability to endure, so that we despaired even of life. Indeed, in our hearts we felt the sentence of death. But this happened that we might not rely on ourselves, but on God, who raises the dead. He has delivered us from such a deadly peril, and he will deliver us. On him we have set our hope that he will continue to deliver us, as you help us by your prayers. Then many will give thanks on our behalf for the gracious favor granted us in answers to the prayers of many."

It was true – all of it. Every word was accurate and believable, fitting every situation, speaking to our hearts when nothing else could. We had felt the sentence of death, but it had forced us to rely on God. He had delivered us, he promised to keep on delivering us, and one day many would praise his matchless name because they had experienced his many answers to prayer in our lives. He could take the worst situation and bring His great good out of it. He had made a promise and he always kept His word.

When I focused on the promises in His Word, He literally renewed my strength and I felt physically lifted on wings of eagles and of angels.

Even on days when I woke wretched and tired, I knew I could lean hard into Him and He would allow me to stand beside James, to wait on him, to help him. Watching James suffer as he tolerated the respirator, the therapists, the blood work and his fatigued muscles was grueling. But every kind nurse, every gentle therapist or considerate doctor was God's reminder that He was with us every step of this journey.

Even something as simple as a Buzz Light Year bank brought us a slice of joy. One of the other parents on the floor presented James with a savings bank which announced "Buzz Light Year to the Rescue!" every time you inserted a coin. The Buzz Light Year figure would raise his arms and make his declaration in a comical voice that delighted James. When Bill suggested, "James, why don't you make every doctor, nurse and therapist who enters your room put a coin in your bank before they can work on you?" James thought the idea inspiring and squealed delightfully at this new escapade. The hospital staff's visits were no longer viewed as a torture session for James; now he could torture them.

But not even a stash of coins could eliminate all the misery. When his left leg, severely compromised by the stroke, turned grotesquely purple, he winced painfully each time the therapist attempted to manipulate it. Unfortunately, an IV line had infiltrated a blood vessel during the last surgery, creating one more aggravating detail to endure. His legs trembled as the therapist and Bill attempted to re-introduce him to the art of standing. He had to reacquaint his body with the simple exercises of sitting and standing because the stroke had sent a message to his brain that it no longer had a left side. Every movement in therapy, every forced exercise, was an attempt to stimulate the brain to the left side's existence. James struggled, aggravated that every movement cost him so dearly.

The ventilator was still his greatest aggravation, however, because it severely limited his ability to communicate. A breathing tube ran from his wind pipe, through his mouth, was taped to his cheek, and connected to the mechanical respirator/ventilator. The machine would help him breathe until he was capable of breathing on his own, but all attempts to wean him off completely had not yet been successful.

Self-pity took up residence on the Fourth of July. All of America was celebrating our country's freedom, and we were locked behind bars in Miami. I physically ached in every bone and muscle. What I would give simply to be home with our children, about the business of caring for their ordinary, everyday needs. Nothing in the CICU was ordinary or everyday. Hot coals in backyard barbecues grilled meats while our lives were being sacrificed in this furnace. The fire suffocated me, extinguishing hope. When James dozed, I retreated to the window seat in the waiting room and gazed hungrily at the brilliant sky and lush tropical scenery below. We were trapped inside, deep inside. How could we ever escape? I kept my eyes fixed on the view, longing, looking, leaning hard into the pane.

In the afternoon a cool breeze blew through. Kathy, Souhila, and Jill arrived with a picnic banquet. Huge take-out plates brimmed high with ribs, fries and slaw and the trio cheered James with gifts of puzzles, videos and even embossed socks with his favorite cartoon characters. Did they even comprehend what their visit and laughter meant? Could we ever thank them enough for coming to help us get past the dreary day? The Fourth found its way inside; fireworks had arrived at last.

Frequently, the doctors described James' condition in dismal terms wrapped in vague apprehension that felt as if I had been asked to chew a glassful of nails, swallow them quickly, and then repeat the painful process. Immediately after digesting one batch of bad news, we were forced to accept another round of difficult diagnoses. Sometimes their words pierced through us like a vacuum cleaner sucking out our insides and then systematically spraying the mess right back into our faces. But when I lived inside God's Word, when I leaned desperately into His strength, I was given grace to swallow nails and handle vacuum cleaners, too. I recorded John 14:27 in my journal as it seemed to leap off the page of my Bible. "Peace I leave with you, my peace I give you. I do not give you as the world gives. Do not let your heart be troubled and do not be afraid." He also spread His peace to little boys with broken hearts and young children who never knew when their parents were coming home.

We experienced His presence as we found delight in the smallest, seemingly insignificant events or accomplishments. On day thirteen in Miami Children's, I listed ten things that we once would have easily taken for granted.

1. James tossed a ball to Bill.
2. He stroked my face with his little hand.
3. He kept his eyes open a little longer.
4. We were able to take a ride in the car with the three older kids.
5. We had ice cream with the kids.
6. We had clean sheets.
7. James' blood pressure remained stable.
8. He moved his left arm slightly.
9. The bruise on his left leg is disappearing.
10. Every second he is alive is an undeserved gift.

Day 14 in the CICU was a banner day for accomplishments. The catheter was pulled out and a feeding tube put in. James had suffered significant weight loss and they wanted to fatten him up with a multi-vitamin drink pack. His left arm moved slightly more during physical therapy and the respiratory specialist weaned him off the ventilator a few more degrees. The medical team continued to run EKGs and Echocardiograms that revealed steady improvements in the strength of his left ventricle.

Ever since we began this journey in 1993, God continually used the Psalms to improve the strength of my own heart. Whenever James rested and nurses slowed their pace and therapists left his room, I would hide myself in the very place King David had found refuge. With all else stripped away, I gathered my parched soul and ran for cover in the pages where I could find the Comforter. The One whom I had come to know intimately as my soul's Good Samaritan would come alongside my dusty road, bend close to pour oil in my wound, bandage my bruises, carry me to an inn and even pay the innkeeper to tend to my needs. Familiar passages like Psalm 18 became brilliantly new as I discovered they told about God rescuing me at great personal cost from death's tightly coiled cords. For the psalmist and for our family, God had swooped down from on high, breaking every barrier, shaking seas, tearing mountains asunder in His heroic rescue. In that tiny CICU room, where I should have been overwhelmed by James' critical condition, I was overwhelmed instead by the Savior's powerful, relentless love. Just as David experienced God as his rescuer from Saul, we knew Him as our rescuer from despair and depression.

In Psalm 18:32-35 I discovered the many ways God prepared me to face the battle he had called me to fight. Many of the passage's descriptions were military terms appropriate for the war we were engaged in. God had armed me with strength, made my way perfect, fashioned my feet like deer feet, enabled me to stand on the heights, trained my hands for battle, given me a shield of victory, sustained me with his right hand, and stooped down to make me great. Each one by itself was sufficient, but when considered together they exceeded every possibly need.

On Sunday, July 13th, 1997, God continued his rescue operation as James was finally freed from his dependence on the ventilator. The monitor suspended above his bed displayed great figures without the aid of any artificial devices. We soared higher than the numbers!

There was nothing artificial, either, in the many lessons God taught us through our undesirable school. My mother-instinct desired to rescue James from his pain; I could not. Regardless of the physically pain it cost him, I had to allow our son to undergo breathing treatments, blood work, respiratory therapy, occupational therapy, physical therapy, EKGs, Echocardiograms, X-rays and CAT scans. I was unwilling to prevent any of these treatments no matter how painful they were for him because each one was directly linked to his recovery. Our eternal Father with his loving parent-heart also desired to rescue men and women from their misery. He had full and complete knowledge of our pain and at the same time He was completely capable of rescuing us from the greatest misery of imprisonment to sin and its accompanying sentence of death. His love for us compelled Him to rescue us and His limitless power enabled Him to bring it about. Because of His perfect love, He would not leave us in the misery of our sin and chose instead to rescue us with His own beloved Son.

Although I was incapable of rescuing James, I used my journal each day to write out prayers for him and the rest of my dear family. On July 17th, 1997, the 24th day in CICU, I wrote:

Father, I pray for James. Pour out Your spirit of mercy and strength on him for he is still so weak. Be his portion, his stronghold and comfort his tired heart. Give him your strength, Lord. Help him to relearn how to sit, to balance, to stand and to walk. Father, I am asking you to rescue him from pain. Relieve him of any more hurt for a while, for he has been through so much. I pray you would cover him with the blood of Christ and I beseech you on his behalf. May his sleep, even now, strengthen and heal him.

God, I pray for the other children as well. Lord, use this tough time to make Billy, Greg and Jacqui resilient. God, I try to teach them all year about you, wanting them to know you intimately and to become more like you. Jesus, use these days to craft your image into their souls. Since I cannot be with them, would you draw them closer to you? May you be their comfort and their security and may you protect them with the blood of Christ.

For our family members who care for them, I pray you would pour out rich blessings on them. Father, give our family back ten-fold, no a hundred-fold, for their graciousness to us. Father, may I never forget their love and their kind compassion on our behalf.

Father, I pray for Bill. Please minister to him, build him up and give him your strength. Help him physically, emotionally and spiritually. Allow him to have meaningful times in your word and use him to do great things for you.

Father, you have asked our whole family to share in the fellowship of your suffering – to know disorder, to live where we do not chose, to be at the mercy of others, to be totally out of control. God, you sent your Son for the express purpose of experiencing great suffering and you have allowed us to taste a tiny bit of what he endured.

Thank you for allowing me to experience my son's suffering and glimpse minutely how you agonized for your own Son. As my friend Kim reminded me, you were incapable of comforting your Son and yet you allow me this privilege that you denied yourself.

In Philippians 1:27 you remind me, "Whatever happens, conduct yourselves in a manner worthy of the gospel of Christ." Whatever happens Lord, may we respond that way. In verse 29 you remind me once more the privilege you have bestowed on us. "For it has been granted to you on behalf of Christ not only to believe on him but also to suffer for him."

The following day, July 18th, was a Mount Everest milestone for they moved James out of the CICU and placed him in a regular room after his four weeks stay in Intensive Care. The twelve feet separating the CICU from the regular cardiac floor could have been a thousand as we triumphantly pushed his bed away from the place where death had drawn painfully close.

Monday, July 21, 1997, 10:00a.m.

Dear James,

You will not remember much of what has transpired; I will never forget.

God has taken us down a dark and dingy tunnel, and we stood shaking in front of the door labeled death. Our hands have been resting on the handle of the door and for brief spells we had to crack the door and smell the horrid odor within. It was a putrid smell, wilting every portion of Daddy and me.

But in His sovereignty, God reached down from on high and barred our entrance into that dreadful room. We could feel His very presence before us, and we knew He spared us entry. As long as we have breath, as long as we can speak and share and talk, we will let the world know of His goodness, His mercy, His sufficiency when we were broken, bare and bloodied from this war.

Son of our love, we may go home tomorrow. They whisper it, but I will not allow myself to believe it as yet. I know you are not yet perfectly whole. I know your left ventricle is still weak and your limbs are in need of therapy, but we gladly, gratefully take you home. You have a long way to go; we are with you every step of the way.

On day 30 of our summer adventure camp, the rumors became reality. We were going home! We gathered in the playroom at 1 p.m. as the nurses and therapists threw James a farewell party with bright balloons, a huge cake and cheerfully wrapped presents. Bill arrived at 2 p.m. and together we filled out the last of the release forms and removed the final bandage. We kissed the nurses farewell, snapped a final picture with Dr. Chang, pushed James' wheelchair to the car, buckled him into the car seat, and drove off victoriously for home. Multitudes had assisted us to victory, and we composed and sent out a poem in an attempt to show our gratefulness.

THE WARRIOR'S SONG

The wounded warrior wandered in, laid his weapons down,
Battered and bruised in battles, his heart now wore the scars,
The cardiac team at Children's brought brilliance to the task,
They moved to mend the soldier, make him new at last.
They placed him on the table, stilled his pulsing heart,
Pried away the stagnant, frail; replacing valve for broken parts.
But daylight turned to darkness beneath the bright spotlights,
The warrior faced new struggles; he had to climb new heights,
With every breath they cheered him, the heroes dressed in green,
With every beat, their hearts leaped,
then sank, then leaped unseen.

Those who loved the fighter stood limply by his side,
They knew the God who promises to lead them and to guide.
"Be still," he told them often, "Do not be afraid.
I am the warrior's master. I will give him aid."

Our God who lights the darkness, who calms the wildest storms,
Who grants us peace for panic, regardless of alarms,
Held the soldier safely, held him close and strong,
Speaking comfort, speaking courage,
For the struggle would take long.
"I am not ready, soldier, for you to travel home,
Stay and fight your battles,
Show good can come from harm."

So gallantly he battled, ferocious was the fight,
Death demanded entrance, God denied the right.
He used the men and women, the heroes dressed in green,
To bring about a miracle, His power clearly seen.
Now the warrior's splendor is greater than before,
Not because he's splendid or mighty with a sword,
But because the loved ones and those who came to see,
Worship with fresh new wonder, the God of gracious mercy.

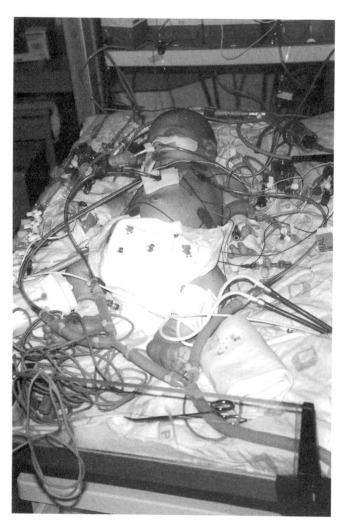

Three days old after first open heart surgery.

Two days after the heart transplant January 1998.

James' Fifth Birthday March 23, 1998,
two months post transplant.

Making friends with our donor mom, Donna Caridi.

Participating in the 2000 US Trasnplant Games.

James with his beloved grandfather.

The Mitchell kids.

Brothers Bill and Greg & Sisters Jacqui and Anna.

Having fun at Awana.

James with his cousins.

On a home school field trip.

Vintage James, First Day of School 2005.

After winning four prizes in a basketball competition.

One of James' passions - basketball at full speed.

CHAPTER 9

CHRISTMAS CRASH

*"I know God will every day show the way to go, and he will direct
my path to the way it should go and I will trust in him and listen
to whatever he has in store for me."*
— *James' Journal Entry, April 29, 2005*

O N Christmas Eve the lights burned out again.
For six months we had helped James recover from the trauma
inflicted by the stroke, the assist device, and by the surgery
itself. With physical therapy and the gradual return to our normal home
school lifestyle, he had regained weight and most of the use of his left
side. James was simply a cheerful, enthusiastic boy who happened to
have congenital heart disease. We continued with his cardiac medications,
routine check-ups with Dr. Rhoden and weekly physical therapy to help
regain movement in his left fingers.

In the early part of December as guests at a cardiac symposium in
Palm Beach, we checked into a lavish hotel, mingled with the doctors,
laughed with the nurses and chatted briefly with Dr. Chang, Dr. Burke
and Dr. Jacobs who all thought James looked wonderful. We stood
before cardiac specialists from around the world and shared a small
portion of what we had experienced as parents on a cardiac intensive
care unit. James was a success story.

But a short-circuited one. On Christmas Eve, right in the midst of all the festivities, James suddenly choked and gasped. A bluish tint brushed his upper lip briefly, and then disappeared. I scrambled for the phone, dialed the cardiologist and the pediatrician, but discovered all offices closed for Christmas.

Hadn't James been doing well? Weren't his check-ups all fine. It was Christmas Eve, after all. We couldn't possibly leave the other children now. Besides, the emergency room was probably packed with holiday mishaps. He would be fine. It was probably nothing, nothing at all.

But it was most certainly something. His pulse registered 140 and never varied throughout the night as he slept restlessly in our bed and we barely closed our eyes. In the morning we attempted bravado for the children as we opened presents, served Christmas breakfast, and pretended desperately that all was well. I interrupted Dr. Rhoden at home and she encouraged us to go to the emergency room.

Christmas was ruined. James was once again in congestive heart failure. The moment we laid him on the bed in the CICU of Miami Children's and the nurse stepped toward him, James wept. He was inconsolable, and I felt like throwing myself down and weeping right alongside him. Dr. Chang ordered a battery of tests that quickly confirmed James' dire condition.

"Remember the option I mentioned this summer? I think we need to reconsider that option now."

How dare he talk to us about options! Didn't he know what we just endured? Didn't he remember how we had struggled for weeks this past summer to get James well? Options! What options now?

With the test results, we were forced to accept that a virus had invaded James' body, attacking and destroying his weakest area – the limping left ventricle. The doctors called it cardiomyopathy, informing us that James' only option was now a heart transplant. No other alternative treatment existed to improve his heart function.

After James finally fell asleep, I hunted for a vacant room to inform my father of the prognosis. "Dad, I can't do this again," I cried into the phone. "So many people have told me I am strong. But I can't do this. I'm weak, completely weak. This can't be happening again! How can James possibly take any more?"

But it was happening, and we were powerless to prevent it. Dread clutched my throat with frost-bitten fingers as the weight of this new diagnosis crushed all our hopes. By New Year's Eve, fear took up permanent residence as the concept of transplants, rejections, and lifelong anti-rejection medications and procedures created a desperate sense of anguish and turmoil. In my head I knew our Heavenly Father loved James immeasurably, but the colossal distractions of despair blocked all my views, leaving behind a panic-filled, dreary landscape in every direction.

Late in the night, at the end of a tiring day with no hope of tomorrow's forecast being brighter, I heard my Aunt Odette's voice on the phone. She did all the talking; exhausted, I could only listen. Besides, I had very little to say anymore. My depleted gut matched my numb brain.

Her gentle, soothing voice began, "Lizzie, I don't want you to fear. In my quiet time this morning God gave me clear assurance that all will be well. I have no fear for James. I want you to rest in His power and trust Him with James." She tucked the words of Psalm 33 into my mind.

"No king is saved by the size of his army; no warrior escapes by his great strength...But the eyes of the Lord are on those who fear him, on those whose hope is in his unfailing love, to deliver them from death and keep them alive in famine" (Psalm 33:16,18).

Engulfed in a famine, facing death, I had to remember the eyes of the Lord were on us and He would in His sovereign time bring deliverance. I must place my hope, my deepest longings, in his unfailing love. He was incapable of failure.

I fled to the bathroom, wept uncontrollably, and asked God's forgiveness for wanting my own way. Fear's tight embrace had squeezed out my belief in his limitless power. Selfishly, I had refused to accept the transplant and had been shaking my fist defiantly in his face, unwilling to surrender my will to his. He knew the best way; I was called to abandon myself and James to him.

For the next two weeks we gradually realized He had re-enrolled us in school to administer another round of tests. Could I trust Him to be the faithful, sovereign Lord He had always proven Himself to be? Was He not tenderly explaining that His ways were not my ways? I must yield my rights to Him: my right to have healthy kids, my right to be with my family, my right to be home, my right to a "normal" life. He knew my deepest longings, my dearest desires. In His time, according to His perfect will, He would accomplish what was best for our family.

He was also teaching me to praise Him, regardless. After all, He had not given me a spirit of fear, but one of power and love and a sound mind (I Timothy 1:7). My fears were like a thousand rats gnawing me; worship music kept the rats at bay. My brother-in-law Rick ransacked his CD collection and compiled a black pouch crammed with beautiful praise and worship albums. Whenever I could turn off the phones and the television, I would slip in a CD and slip away from despair. The songs washed over me, cleansed me, and filled me with strength. One tune particularly positioned itself in my thoughts and paraded its truth continuously. "God will make a way, when there seems to be no way, He works in ways we cannot see, And He will make a way for me..." He was making the way for us. Perhaps we couldn't see it yet, but we could know with absolute assurance that He was making a way for James and for us.

He was also teaching me that I must decrease and He must increase. Our insurmountable circumstances perfectly displayed our weaknesses and our lack of control, but they also forced us to see His limitless strength and our utter dependence on him. Had He not already provided for every need by using our extended family and our church family to under-gird us? Each one had physically and tangibly come alongside to carry our burdens on their own backs and lived through our crisis as if it were their own.

On Friday, January 9, 1998, James began throwing up with each cough. He lost his appetite and withdrew into a pale, listless shadow with all his sparkle dimmed. Dr. Chang and Dr. Burke worked on the details of listing James for transplant, trying to decide whether to perform it in Miami or in Gainesville or Tampa. Every place outside of Miami sounded like the dark side of the moon, but we would have to take that long-distance trip because not one of the brilliant medical minds could eliminate his heart racing at 140 beats per minute, much less repair his heart failure.

Late in the evening, after a large circle of friends joined a challenge to fast and pray through the day for James, something incredible occurred. On a whim, the charge doctor on duty asked the pacemaker specialist to evaluate James before attending to another patient primed for her pacemaker replacement surgery. When he placed the magnet on James' chest, temporarily switching off his pacemaker, James own heart rate escalated to 300 beats per minute. He had been in atrial flutter since Christmas Eve without it being discovered. The efficient pacemaker had masked his true heart rate.

On Saturday the team scheduled James for a standard procedure to place electrical paddles over his heart and shock its rhythm back to normal. Normally, this process is uncomplicated, but nothing was simple with James. The calendar read January 10; his heart had been in atrial flutter for 17 days. Imprisoned in the holding area, every agonizing minute stretched endlessly while dragon-sized flies created havoc in my gut.

James' lips and skin wore no color when he returned; even the soles of his feet bore a pasty yellow tint. A team of doctors, nurses, and technicians encircled his bed, rousing him from anesthesia, monitoring his vital signs, luring him away from death's doorway. His unstable breathing, irregular heart rate, erratic blood pressure and chalky white skin affirmed his apparent destination.

Gradually, James stabilized. I gathered my toiletry bag, searched for an available shower and cried for a long time. I wept for our tiny warrior, forced to endure such adversities. I wept for the unknown and all the uncertainties ahead. I lingered at length in that steamy, solitary shower; it wasn't my skin that needed the cleansing.

The night grew cruel, inflicting further assault on our helpless son. At midnight his IV line disconnected and he cried out in terrified gasps knowing more needle pricks were next. Twice, the nurse attempted to reinsert the line, but his collapsed veins made her job impossible. I draped my body over his to help hold him still, but I longed to stretch out my arm and beg, "Put the needle here! I'll take the pain for him. Don't hurt him anymore. I can't bear to have you hurt him anymore."

Instead, I bit my lip; my tears rolled out quietly. His sobs shook the bed. Finally at 2 a.m., after two excruciating hours, the specialized IV nurse appeared and placed the new line within minutes. James drifted off to sleep; I lay awake for a very long time.

In hospitals, Sundays bring no rest. In the afternoon, the nurses gave James a sedative, and I was glad to see him giggle in his "intoxicated" state. They decided to place a PIC line into his arm, a larger tube than the IV line and one which was usually permanent. James was not pleased with this new idea and the sedative was ineffective in dulling his senses. Three of us held him down as he fought like a trapped tiger. I clutched him and prayed silently, "God, I beg you. Give James courage for this too. Give the nurse extra skill in placing this PIC line."

It went in easily.

As the team completed its task, a ring of nurses and doctors encircled the three-week-old infant in the next unit. His mother, Carol, had never even held her son, born on Christmas Eve. She had recently shared with me her fears of the months of suffering still ahead as together they would have to fight this battle of congenital heart disease without any assurance of the outcome.

Moments later, they drew the curtain around his cubicle. The charge nurse poked her head into our unit. "Mrs. Mitchell, do you mind going to talk to Carol next door? No one is with her and I think you could help."

I approached timidly. What could I possibly say to comfort this grieving mother? "I'm so sorry you never got to hold your baby," I said after first placing my arms around her and holding her.

"They just now allowed me to," she replied. "Somehow, it just wasn't the same."

And for her nothing would ever be the same again. Her little boy was finished with his pain, but hers would continue indefinitely. Two little boys with their beds only two feet apart; James lay far too close to death.

On Tuesday, January13th, the team discussed the need for a feeding tube for James. His scrawny limbs protruded pitifully beneath his cartoon-covered hospital gown, but I dreaded this next act of intervention, knowing how James would despise this new invasion. His labored breathing brought the chest physiotherapist (CPT) to administer breathing treatments, clapping his back repeatedly to dislodge and remove the secretions in his lungs. James sighed every time they approached, but sat bravely, submitting to the necessary torture. He gently accepted whatever they forced him to endure.

During the treatment, I pressed myself against the small window in the CICU cubicle, looking at the lush landscape beneath and the brilliant blue canopy overhead. Everything outside that window represented freedom from our prison cell, and I ached to gallop away to safety with James in my arms. But as I peered longingly outside, the Lord filled my thoughts with a verse. "For as high as the heavens are above the earth, so great is His love for those who fear him" (Psalm 103:11). Now the view could no longer remind me of what I could not possess; God reminded me of all I had. Triumph in a prison cell.

We knew triumphs in others ways as well. Once I implored God for mercy, begging him to show us his mercy that day. Imagine my delightful surprise when the nursing student came into the room and introduced herself. "Hello, my name is Mercy. I'm here to help with James today."

God had simply thought to send us a pretty picture postcard.

It was thrilling to view God at work right before our eyes. Every time the nurses changed shifts I remembered Paul's delight in the book of Philippians. Because of being chained to a variety of palace guards,

Paul was able to preach the gospel to a multitude he could reach no other way. God had us in this hospital for His purpose, and with each shift we had the opportunity to impact a whole new group of people for His kingdom's sake. Few things could match the privilege of sharing Christ, and He had provided us with both the time and the audience. God brought triumph from a prison cell for Joseph and for Paul. He could do it with us as well.

In His faithfulness, God was slowing chipping away my resistance to the transplant. He brought me a mother whose child had undergone a transplant two years earlier, and I drank in the pictures of her beautiful, normal daughter. Later, we met a 12-year-old boy from the Cayman Islands who had received a heart transplant at Miami Children's the year before. His angelic face and charming spirit captivated me. Both children were beautiful; both children had had heart transplants.

The social worker began the tedious process of evaluating our family to determine whether or not we truly were emotionally and psychologically prepared to handle this excruciating process. We filled out reams of official forms and endured hours of analysis as they scrutinized our family structure and support systems, our financial resources, and basically our ability to cope with the dramatic, relentless battering we would have to endure before, during and after the transplant. They wanted to resolve all doubts about James' "candidacy for transplantation."

Along with his routine Electrocardiograms (EKG), Echocardiogram (ultrasounds of the heart) and chest x-rays, James also had to undergo daily blood and urine samplings. The urine tests would determine whether his kidneys and liver had the healthy stamina to handle the enormous volume of medications required for transplant. The blood work was to confirm his blood type and grouping, his antigen and antibody reactions, his tissue typing and thyroid function.

But perhaps the hardest part was waiting without any idea of when, or if, a viable heart would ever be available. We discovered Miami Children's had only performed one heart transplant to date and that it was trying to partner with nearby Jackson Memorial Hospital to coordinate all the details for the transplantation. But could James' own heart survive until all the processes came together? Would a new heart arrive in time?

CHAPTER 10

FLIGHT FOR FREEDOM

"If we call to God, He will save us."

— James' Journal Entry, November 1, 2004

I needed to hear the Father's voice.

On Wednesday, January 14, 1998, amidst the hectic CICU, I hid in a vacant corner, pulled out my journal and wrote, "Father, hide me in your stillness here in this noisy place. Give James this day your supernatural ability to endure – to sense your power and your might as a strong, secure presence around him. Lord, I pray you would increase his appetite, pick up his spirits, and blow your healing breath into his lungs and heart. Father, I know that if you did not want us here, we would not be in this place. I know that when you no longer want us here, you will take us away. Help me to rest in that truth."

Everywhere I turned in the Scriptures I was confronted by the theme that suffering for Christ was an honorary privilege. In Acts 5:41 I read, "The apostles left the Sanhedrin rejoicing because they had been counted worthy of suffering disgrace for the Name." Peter and the other apostles had just been flogged and scolded, and they went out rejoicing. In Philippians 1:29 Paul tells us, "For it has been granted to you on behalf of Christ not only to believe on him, but also to suffer for him." The word *granted* clearly showed suffering for Christ as a distinguished honor. James was not suffering for his own sake. We were not suffering for our sake. No, we were Christ's ambassadors, suffering on His behalf, suffering for His purposes.

Thursday, January 15th, began timidly, and I slipped outside for a walk while James slept. The frail, newborn girl in the unit beside us was being disconnected from her assist device and the entire CICU was in commotion as the team prepared to perform the procedure in her room. I chatted with the family briefly and felt it best to leave the unit for a while. I passed Dr. Chang in the hall and nodded a brief hello before entering the elevator. The charming Coral Gables neighborhood around the hospital was a perfect setting for praying aloud, listening, and praising. I walked fast, relishing the fresh air and admiring the quaint homes.

During my one-hour walk I implored the Lord for His will to be done in our lives. I urgently sensed God at work among us orchestrating our present situation for far-reaching effects. We were simply privileged to be allowed a part in what He was accomplishing.

I returned to the unit rejuvenated but immediately noticed Dr. Jacobs slumped by a desk and the nurses' agitation. The curtain drawn around the little girl's cubicle could not muffle the sobbing sounds. It had happened again, this time on our right side. Two tiny babies had now died on each side of us. Death pressed its ugly face closer.

I pulled our curtain closed, but moments later my brother Paul entered with coffee and a breakfast muffin. He had left work to bring by a treat and cheer up James. His timing was perfect. He visited for an hour, hugged me tightly, and left the curtain of our cubicle slightly opened. I glanced at the nurse's station outside James' doorway and spotted Dr. Chang's eyes on us. I immediately looked away. Perhaps he thought I was prying into our neighbor's situation and would ask me to leave. Each patient's privacy was top priority on that unit.

Dr. Chang strode over to our door and beckoned me into the hall. Joanne, the nurse practitioner, stood beside us. I held my breath. "Sometimes we take a long time to make decisions," he began, "but I told you before, once I make up my mind, we move fast."

I was unprepared for what came out next. "I want James to go to Gainesville today. We are processing all the paperwork now. Can you be ready to go in an hour?"

Joanne reached for my elbow as I staggered backward. "I thought we were doing the transplant here," I mumbled. "I thought he was already listed, and we were preparing to do it here in Miami."

"I don't want James to be entangled in hospital bureaucracy," Dr. Chang explained. "Unfortunately, in large hospitals red tape causes delays. I don't want to take that chance with James." He turned and walked away.

I stumbled toward the phone to inform Bill. My tongue stuck to the roof of my mouth and the words caught in my cotton-lined throat as I explained the situation. When I hung up, paralysis glued me to the chair. *What do I do now? Vivian! I'll go to Vivian.*

Vivian's son Anthony was a frequent patient on the CICU floor and we had grown attached to each other. Anthony's severe deformities forced them to spend months of his life in many of the hospital units. Vivian's smile betrayed no self pity; her face was marked by a brilliant beauty found in the secret place of acceptance.

She saw my confusion, heard the story and held me. "Vivian, they are sending James to Gainesville, and they've told me it's not likely I can fly with him in the helicopter."

"Elizabeth, whatever they tell you, you insist that you must fly with James. Insist on it. You must be beside him." Her voice was a call to courage.

"I need to pack all his things. Do you have a bag I can borrow?" I left Vivian's room with a duffel bag under my arm and a steadfast determination to be packed before they came for us. My brother Paul, half way home when he heard the sudden change in plans, returned to my side and carted James' newly acquired collection of games, puzzles, videos and stuffed animals to his car. The helicopter would allow no extra weight.

"Honey, we have to take a little trip," I explained to James as he watched me dismantle the room. "We are going on an adventure, you and Mummy."

"I don't want to go anywhere. Come sit with me. I don't want to go." His voice trembled and he pulled his hair between his fingers.

"James, sweetie, it's going to be OK. Mummy has to pack up all our things. I'll sit with you in a little."

But in a little, the orange transport team slammed into the space outside our room like a gigantic freight train. No time left to pack, think or sit. Bill and the children were on the highway, barreling down to Miami, and we would have to leave them without saying goodbye.

James whimpered as the orange team transferred him to the skinny gurney and reconnected his IVs to portable units. My breathing came in tight, squeezed puffs. This was happening fast, way too fast. Time was running out.

The medics tightened the safety straps around James and began pushing the gurney toward the elevator when Bill and the children tumbled out the open elevator doors. They had made it. Suddenly, all three grandparents arrived, and we quickly encircled his cot, holding hands in prayer. When I opened my eyes, all the nurses, now our dearest friends, were crying softly around us.

We boarded the helicopter and flew. James knew no fear. He was perfectly content because I was beside him. From his point of view, the 3,000 feet-high ride was no big deal. The 300 mile distance between Gainesville and Miami never bothered him in the least. His mother was beside him, and he was happy. When would I learn this vital lesson from my tiniest teacher? My Father, too, stood beside me, and it should be irrelevant to me how far away I was from home. In just the way I willingly, eagerly cared for James in his weakened state, my Father willingly, eagerly, lovingly would care for me at every stage of our adventure, regardless of how weak I felt.

All this ran through my mind, crept into the deepest crevices of my thoughts as I relived the journey from the beginning, all the way back to this Gainesville hotel room across the road from the place where we would now wait, perhaps indefinitely, for a brand new heart for James. The memories held me hostage all night.

In the morning, the adventure quickly intensified as the computer screen registered Friday, January 16, 1998, as James' first official day listed on the United Network of Organ Sharing (UNOS). The transplant coordinator, Kelli Harker, explained that James' case would receive top priority in our region. Due to his critical condition, he would be the first one selected to receive a heart from any matching donor in the southeastern region of the United States.

"Kelli, how long do patients wait before getting a heart?" I asked tentatively.

"Well, it all depends on how sick the child is," she replied in a matter-of-fact tone. "Usually, the wait is between several weeks and a few months. But if he's sick enough, he'll get bumped up."

Once listed, we were also candidates for one of the furnished apartments close to Shands rented at a significant discount to transplant families. We appraised the apartment, bought necessary linens, stocked the fridge and prepared for our other children's arrival the following day. Bill's parents would bring them and their home-school supplies to Gainesville because I felt that if we were together I could perhaps endure the long grueling weeks ahead.

In the afternoon we met Tricia, the 16-year-old in the room next to James, who had been at Shands for two weeks waiting for her heart. She pushed her IV pole beside her and brought candies to welcome her new neighbor.

James' entire outlook brightened at Shands. With the PIC line still implanted in his arm, he was free from continuous poking and pricking since all blood samples and medications were processed through the PIC line. Each dose of medicine prodded his worn out pump to continue the fight. The dark circles which rimmed his eyes and his skinny limbs could not distract from his robust spirit and sunshine smile. Just as he had done in Miami, he began to win the hearts of the Shands team. He radiated a joy undimmed by his circumstance because the Lord who asked him to endure great difficulties also gave him a mighty spirit to overcome. He looked perfectly content as he sipped Gatorade, munched snacks and operated the television control like a pro. We passed the time by playing card games which he always seemed to win, his sense of competition still fierce despite his bedridden state.

We were watching an "Arthur" video at 9 p.m. when a nurse entered to report, "Tricia next door asked me to let you know she's getting her heart tonight." Her excitement radiated through the wall and I slipped into her room to offer congratulations. While the nurse drew vials of blood in preparation for the surgery, I chatted with Tricia's mom, a fellow pilgrim on a journey for the heart. Tricia's face glowed, radiant as a bride looking forward to her wedding day.

CHAPTER 11

"WE HAVE A HEART FOR JAMES"

"If you trust in God, he will lead you to victory."
— James' Journal Entry, September 10, 2004

ON Saturday morning we woke early, eager to return to James and excited for the other children's arrival. We had spent the night in the Ronald McDonald House close to the hospital, housed with strangers hundreds of miles away from our children and millions of miles away from a solution to our problem. While we waited for visiting hours to begin, Bill made business calls and I chatted with other parents in the kitchen.

The beautiful home with its gracious amenities had been built to make weary parents comfortable while their children faced critical battles at Shands. One father eased back in his chair and told me his story.

Returning from vacation, a horrible car accident a few miles from Gainesville had lacerated their family. Their car had flipped and everyone catapulted out safely except his 17-year-old son, trapped beneath the vehicle. Truck drivers appeared like angels across the horizon and lifted the car off his son's body. Now he lay critically burnt, his entire face and upper chest scorched. They had already been at the Ronald McDonald House for three weeks, living out the agony with their son as he came to terms with his disfigured teenage face.

His grief sat between us like a blackened boulder. "Don't you just wish you could just carry your son's pain for a little while?" I asked.

He looked back at me with eyes that had seen too much suffering. "No. I wish I could just give him my face."

Our conversation ended; nothing more could be said. His words played a haunting refrain the rest of the day. Somewhere, I had heard a similar tune. Wasn't that the eternal song the Father had played for us with His own beloved Son? God looked down from on high and saw our misery and sin. God ached for our hopelessness, and his Father-heart wanted to carry our pain. So, Jesus came. He had his body scorched on the cross just so He could give us His face. Jesus came to give us His own face, His own life, His own blood. Take-out lessons at Ronald McDonald's don't always get served with a smile.

At four o' clock that afternoon I walked down a hospital corridor in search of a laundry room with our dirty clothes spilling out of a torn plastic bag. I turned a corner and before me stood a beautiful sight: Billy, Gregory and Jacqui. I dropped the bag and squealed.

Throughout the weekend, we relayed between the apartment and the hospital, tending to James and attempting to help the children feel at home in their new surroundings. Bill gave each of us an extra long hug and climbed into the car to return to his job Monday morning. I woke up in our new apartment missing my husband desperately and reached for the phone before it could wake the kids. My father had called to encourage me with a devotional from "Streams in the Dessert." I heard my Heavenly Father's voice through his, calling early in the morning to remind me of his love. I was utterly convinced my dad would move heaven and earth to provide for his family's needs. My Heavenly Father, who could literally move heaven and earth on our behalf, was more than willing and able.

James received an overdue haircut in his bed that afternoon and his little face appeared less gaunt. Bill called all through the day, eager to hear updates. His body was in Boca, but his heart was with us in Gainesville.

"Dr. Fricker wants to catherize James tomorrow," I relayed. "They are deeply concerned about the elevated pressure in his lungs, and they also want to take a closer look at his heart."

"Will it be risky?"

"Not normally. This is a simple procedure," I explained. "But Dr. Fricker knows James. They are going to avoid anesthesia if at all possible." My stomach performed somersaults as I continued. "If the pressures are too high, they are going to put James on a ventilator until the transplant."

Bill was quiet, understanding how tedious this would be for his son. To wait weeks or even months for a heart was one thing. But it would be close to intolerable for James if he was strapped to a ventilator.

We turned to less suffocating thoughts. "Our first day of school went fairly well," I encouraged him. "Your mom went to the hospital this morning, and I stayed in and worked with the kids."

"How was it?"

"Okay. We'll just do what we have to for a while."

"This might take weeks and weeks, you know."

"I know."

When he called back at five in the afternoon I reported, "Some days fly by and some linger indefinitely. This was a long one. But James looks okay, better than he has for weeks." I was glad to share some good news for a change.

They prepared James for his heart catheterization and wheeled him away at noon on Tuesday. I was allowed to suit up in a sterile gown and mask and escort James into the lab, standing by his gurney until the anesthesia took effect as they prepared this tiny soldier for another battlefield. In the waiting room I wrote out a prayer:

"Father, even now as they would enter his body for this procedure, do what seems best to you. Father, hold him now in the very center of your palm; keep him in the shadow of your wings. Give the doctors wisdom they never knew they possessed. Lord, if he needs to go on the ventilator, would you give him the grace not to be frustrated. Even now Lord, would you cover him with your breastplate of

righteousness, the shield of faith, the belt of truth, and the sword of the Spirit. Prepare him for the battle as only you can do."

The battle heated up quickly. I glimpsed Dr. Fricker's face and I jumped to greet him. "He did all right," he spoke reassuringly. "The pressures are not as high as we anticipated, and so he won't need a respirator."

I released a sigh as the load rolled off my tense shoulders.

He turned to leave, halted, and then resumed, "Mrs. Mitchell. I hesitate to tell you this because I'm not sure of the details, but I think it best to inform you that we've been notified of a possible heart for James."

He had my full attention. "We are uncertain if the heart is viable or not. There are some problems with it, and we do not know if it will work. I don't want to give you false hope but ...."

I smiled. The mere possibility of a heart being available so soon after our arrival was mind boggling. "When will you know for sure?" I asked.

"Around four o' clock, I think."

But at four o'clock there was no sign of Dr. Fricker, and I was consumed with caring for James. The after-effects of the anesthesia caused him to vomit every 15 minutes. His tiny frame was a pitiful sight as he thrashed up and down on the bed, trying to find a comfortable spot. I held him, rocked him, stroked his back, but nothing made him comfortable. In desperation, he finally threw himself against the bottom of his bed, curled his legs beneath him and fell asleep. Mom, Jacqui and I sat limply beside his bed, unable to move for a while.

"I need some fresh air," I told them. "Let's go home and check on the boys while James sleeps."

Mom began preparations for spaghetti and I curled up on the sofa with all three kids for a history lesson. The phone rang and I jumped. "Mrs. Mitchell, this is Kelli."

"Yes Kelli."

"We have a heart for James!"

"Are you sure? Should I call my husband?"

"Yes. Call him right away. We're 98 percent certain it's a match. See if he can arrive before surgery."

I did not cry or scream; I just stood mesmerized beside the wall phone, my lungs tight. "They have a heart for James," I announced. "I need to reach Daddy." Mom rested the cooking spoon down and cried. I called Bill.

But I couldn't find him. He was not in his office and not in cell phone range. I redialed his office, reached his secretary and explained, "Rita. I need to find Bill. It's very important. Can you help me?" My voice shook with each word.

Moments later Bill called back. "Bill, they've found a heart for James. They say they are 98 percent certain it's a match. You need to come right away."

"I'll get there as soon as I can. This is what we've been waiting for, right?"

"Right!"

My heart banged in gigantic thumps and I called the children together. "Billy, will you stay with Gregory while Jacqui comes with Mimi and me?" Gregory was fighting the stomach flu and Billy had been his side-kick these past few days.

We huddled close and prayed, "Father, we commit James to you. Help him make it through this surgery. Protect the boys at the apartment. Help Daddy get here soon."

I squished the boys against me in the tightest possible hug, turned the key in the lock, and marched out to join the tiny warrior.

CHAPTER 12

WAITING ROOM DRAMA

"The LORD can help you when you are weak, and He can help you when you are strong."
— James' Journal Entry, September 30, 2004

W E found the soldier pouting, restless and irritable. Nothing we did or said helped and at 6:15 p.m. the nurse finally administered a sedative. He threw up again, the continuing anesthesia after-effects, thrashed from one end of the bed to the other, and eventually fell asleep in my arms. I held him tight, his naked frame clothed in a skimpy hospital gown, and rocked him back and forth. I prayed aloud then, wrapped our golden-haired angel within my arms and simply prayed.

"Thank you, Father, for everything you have done for James from Bethesda hospital to Boston to Jackson to Miami Children's to right now. Father, may your glory overwhelm the operating room. Give each one who touches James a supernatural skill far beyond their own natural ability.

"God, would you take the surgeon's hands in yours and be the one to open James' chest, remove his weary heart, and replace it with a strong and healthy one. You be the one to cut through all those layers of scar tissue that will be in the way."

It was after eight in the evening when they came to take James from my arms. While I held him, the anesthesiologists and three other doctors brought release forms needing my signature. Each of them, in turn, shared every conceivable problem that could transpire during the transplant surgery. I nodded, refusing to believe their grim news, and signed each form with James still perched on my lap. Nightmares paled in comparison. A new heart for James might come at a higher price than we could even conceive.

Dr. Joelle Miller, the cardiologist who first diagnosed James on the day he was born, called from Virginia while we were waiting for the team to transport James to the OR. "I heard the news from Dr. Chang. I had to call right away. James is going to do beautifully. I just know it."

"Dr. Miller, you've been with us since the beginning of all this, haven't you?"

"He's a good boy. He's going to do well. I just know he will."

We walked beside his gurney, three women who adored our tiny brave warrior, and watched his chariot rumble quietly into the OR. The waiting room was deathly still. Forty-something empty, plastic chairs mocked us. If we were closer to home, every chair and every inch of flooring would be jammed with our family and church friends, but God had written this portion of the symphony for three instruments only. I hugged Jacqui, held Mom's hand, and knew the empty seats were a lie. God had gone ahead of us, and this barren waiting room was filled with the presence of the Almighty. He was enough. He was always enough.

Bill was barreling north with my brother Kary and called constantly for updates. The surgical coordinator made brief appearances, giving us sketchy progress reports. I tried to read the Psalms but felt restless and paced the hallway instead. We could not reach Billy or Greg by phone, and I began to imagine all the worst scenarios possible: strange town, tiny apartment, two young boys, no family in town to call and check on them, no way to leave the hospital to see how they were doing. With each busy signal, the panic within me multiplied. *Not tonight! Not tonight of all nights. How can I possibly carry any more?*

The elevator signal rang and I looked down the hall at four people striding toward us. Perhaps they, too, had a child in surgery. But, no,

I recognized one face – Kathi Moonie, a friend of my cousin. Kathi had called us the day after we arrived in Gainesville and asked, "What can the family of God in Gainesville do for you?" Since then she had stocked our kitchen with cooking supplies, brought us meals, helped me locate the library and parks for the kids and had been an all-round genuine angel of mercy.

"Kathi, I'm worried about the boys. I can't get through to them on the phone and I can't leave to check on them," I blurted out.

"Oh, don't worry about them," she replied soothingly. "The four of us just stopped by the apartment and brought them a gallon of chocolate ice cream. They're perfectly fine."

Our four new friends kept us company until 10:30 p.m. when Bill and Kary arrived. The cavalry had come through.

But the clock stood still. We heard no reports from the operating room and saw no one in the corridors. By midnight my legs turned to noodles and ice surged through my veins. *Why couldn't someone come with an update? Something dreadful must have happened! James was not doing well, and they were afraid to let me know. Two hours had passed without one word from the OR. How could they be so thoughtless?*

Finally, the coordinator entered the room at 12:30 p.m. and spoke in the calmest tones. "James is doing well. The new heart is being sutured into place. He's off the heart-lung machine."

We jumped out of our seats, hugged each other and laughed out loud. We bombarded her with questions but she quickly slipped away, leaving us one more important bit of news: we could phone the OR anytime for updates.

Jacqui's eyes were drooping shut and Kary volunteered to take her to the apartment. Her bright, cheerful attitude had comforted me throughout our critical ordeal. Not once had this seven-year-old complained about the time, the wait, or the uncertainty. Instead, she splashed sunshine into that drab waiting room. She was my steady companion, a gift God gave me that I desperately needed.

I thought, too, of my brave Billy at the apartment tending to his brother, and I knew that God would somehow reward each of them for the sacrifices they had made for James. They had lived through one challenging crises after another during the past four years. Too often we had no alternative but to leave them for lengthy periods as we cared for James. Too often they had felt the surge of insecurity when they were made aware of the critical nature of his illness. With all the attention focused on James, all the fuss and hoopla revolving around his latest illness or dramatic recovery, it could have been tedious for them.

But I knew the same Lord who had given Bill and me the grace to endure was also providing for our three older children. I knew He was aware of any sacrifice He had asked them to make, and He would pour sensitivity, courage, and great faith into their own souls as rewards. Whatever was meant for evil, God would always turn for great good. He was carving His character into their personalities, and I welcomed His handiwork in their lives.

At 3 a.m. we were allowed to see our little boy with his new heart. They transported him to the Cardiovascular Intensive Care Unit on the second floor and placed him in a private room. We entered cautiously and were pleasantly surprised. He was not bloated, and there were far fewer IV lines and complicated machines attached to him than after his previous surgeries. The green-screened monitors flashed with his blood pressure, heart rate, breathing and oxygen levels. The numbers were stable, and he looked as if he were merely taking a nap.

"He's doing marvelous!" The nurses beamed and chattered excitedly. "He really went through his surgery well. He's perfectly stable and responding right on cue."

What lovely words.

A breathing tube extended out of his mouth, across his cheek and connected to a ventilator. This mechanical respirator breathed for James while he was in surgery and would be in place until he was strong enough to breathe on his own. A plastic nasogastric (NG) tube had been inserted into his stomach and curled out of his nose and into a transparent container in order to prevent air and fluids from collecting in his stomach.

He wore a loose diaper and we could clearly see the elongated incision which ran from his breast bone down to his navel. The incision was held together by a dozen silver staples covered with a transparent bandage. Below the incision, two flexible, plastic tubes extended from his skin. Their purpose was to prevent air and fluid from collecting inside his chest and to enable his lungs to expand. Patches the size of silver dollars were stuck to his shoulders and sides. They connected to an EKG above the bed that monitored his heart rate. A small rubber catheter coiled from the diaper to a collection bag on the side of the bed. In order to check the function of his kidneys, his urine would be collected and measured every hour. On each arm there were two intravenous catheters or IVs to measure his blood pressure, insert medications and collect blood without needlessly sticking him.

"We'll be checking his temperature, urine output and all his vital signs every hour. Don't you worry! We have all your phone numbers. We'll call you if you need to come back. But he's going to be asleep for a while. You've all had a long night. Why don't you head on home and get a little rest? Come back fresh in the morning. He'll be fine. You'll see." The cheerful nurses encouraged us without once breaking stride as they maneuvered around James.

We nodded, exited the CICU and collided with the surgeon, Dr. James Alexander, in the hallway. Dr. Alexander looked more like a cowboy than a surgeon and spoke with swaggering confidence. "The old heart was difficult to retrieve and was almost unrecognizable because of how enlarged and flabby it had become. Peeling away the scar tissue took much longer than we anticipated because of all the surgeries he had already endured."

"How large was his heart?" Bill asked.

Dr. Alexander cupped both his oversized palms together. "About this size - and that was just the ventricle. We cut out the ventricle, but left the atrium behind in order to stitch the new heart onto it. Have you ever tried to pry away bologna from a two-day-old sandwich? You know how the bologna is stuck fast to the bread? That's how messed up his heart was. It was stuck to everything!"

I didn't think I'd ever be able to eat a bologna sandwich again.

CHAPTER 13

SELFLESS SACRIFICE

"If we are truthful we will save lives and be a blessing to others."
-James' Journal Entry, February 23, 2005

I am not easily impressed and I am very impressed with your little boy." The nurse beamed at us when we returned later that morning. "He's a good boy."

James skin glowed and his face radiated health. I glowed, too.

Dr. Chang called from Miami sounding pleased as well. He was astounded that James received the heart just four days after being placed on the List. "What timing!" he exclaimed. "James is a very lucky boy!"

"Dr. Chang," I interjected. "You know it's not luck. God's in control here. He has been from the beginning."

"Well."

"Do you mind if I ask you a question, Dr. Chang?"

"Go ahead."

"What prompted you to rush us off so quickly last Thursday? What made you send us to Gainesville so suddenly?"

"I don't know," he replied thoughtfully. "I just had a feeling."

As the day progressed I discovered the donor heart had been retrieved at 8:20 p.m. and placed in James' chest three hours and forty-one minutes later. A surgical team, called the "donor team" or "away team", flew from Shands to the other hospital, and while Dr. Alexander was in the midst of cutting through James' scar tissue, they retrieved the donor heart, placed it in a cooler and flew back to Shands. James officially received his heart at 12:01 a.m., Wednesday, January 21, 1998. The optimum time lapse between retrieving and implanting is four hours. James made it with 19 minutes to spare.

The hospital would provide no information about the donor family because everything regarding the details of the heart was strictly confidential. We could write a letter of gratitude if we chose, and it would be forwarded to the family on our behalf.

But the news of James' transplant erupted exactly as the newspapers were jammed with the story of a young girl's tragic death. On Monday, January 19, 1998, Veray Caridi of Davie, Florida was accidentally shot by her older sister when they discovered their father's pistol in the master bedroom closet. Veray was eight years old, her sister was 12. They were home alone on Monday because of the official holiday for Martin Luther King, Jr.'s birthday. Davie was 30 minutes from our home in Boca Raton and every local newspaper and news station carried the unfortunate story, including the fact that all the organs had been flown to Shands Hospital in Gainesville.

Simultaneously, we discovered more details that confirmed the origin of James' heart. Dr. Donna Rhoden, James' cardiologist in Boca, had a partner named Kathy Welch who was called to Broward General Hospital to determine if an eight-year old girl's heart was viable for transplant. She proceeded with her examination and necessary tests and called Dr. Rhoden.

"Donna, you need to sit down," Dr. Welch exclaimed. "We have a heart for James! It has his name written all over it!"

Later Dr. Welch filled in the particulars. The Shand's surgical team, eager to return to Gainesville, had no desire to wait for the traumatized heart to recover. Time was everything. The other organs had to be harvested and flown out immediately. "But I begged them to wait," Dr. Welch said. "I told them I knew where the heart was going, I knew who the recipient was, and that they just had to give me a little more time to medicate and stabilize the heart." Her appeal won and they waited for the medications to take effect. The organs were harvested; the heart was the last one to leave.

As each of these descriptions filtered through, we were fully convinced that God had orchestrated the details to reveal our exact donor family. Our family and church had been praying for them from the moment we realized James' need for a heart transplant. Before James could ever have his surgery, some family somewhere would face an inconsolable loss. We prayed earnestly for God to use us in some way to comfort and encourage them.

Thursday, January 22, 1998, 6:30 a.m.

Dear Heavenly Father,

I am grateful you would wake me early before the day galloped off at full speed. I am thankful for the privilege of being in a quiet room with my family sleeping close by. I praise you for a great night of sleep. I praise you for keeping James safe and secure throughout the night without any calls from the hospital.

I praise you for today, Lord. I do not know what it will hold. I know you hold us and you hold James and you hold this day. I praise you that I can come boldly into your presence with empty hands for you to fill. I come to you for you are my Father and I truly have no one else and no where else to go.

I praise you for demonstrating your power in our lives. I praise you for knowing all and understanding all the details. I praise you for being faithful and for not allowing my doubts and fears to affect your faithfulness. I am in awe of you for taking pity on us, showing us great compassion, and pouring over us buckets of your mercy.

Today I ask you to tear down any strongholds of fear and doubt in my life. Would you remove all my anxious thoughts and bring every thought of mine under the obedience of Jesus Christ.

At 9:30 a.m. I checked in at the nurse's station and received approval to enter the CICU area. The nurse's reports were all positive. He was weaned off two medications and the Nitric Oxide he had been receiving for the elevated pressures in his lungs was disconnected. If he continued to do well, they planned to take him off the ventilator, less than 48 hours after transplant.

The thrilling update was mirrored on our patient's face. Even though tubes, wires and bandages covered his body, he did not appear sickly. Rather, his skin glowed golden like a tawny lion cub and it was apparent the Lion of Judah had indeed breathed out His healing power on our son.

The efficient nurses treated James gently and when Kelli appeared she reported, "Many people are impressed with your son. The anesthesiologist who was encouraging him to count backward so they could help him fall asleep was amazed that James knew all his numbers and could say the alphabet backward as well." They were all drawn to James not realizing that thousands of loving people were praying for him continuously. The unique quality they sensed around James was the touch of the Holy Spirit's presence.

His nurses at Miami Children's had also been strongly affected by James. They still called him by his nickname of "Jamers" and sent a touching e-mail conveying their resounding congratulations. When I spoke with Joanne by phone she relayed that the entire unit erupted in hoots and hollers when the news of James' new heart was announced.

The celebrations continued in the afternoon when James was disconnected from the ventilator and his entire, adorable face was visible once more. He looked beautiful and healthy, but a bit perturbed at his menu options. "Can I have some apple juice, water, milk or anything?" he pleaded. Dr. Alexander was adamant that no excess fluids of any kind should tax the new heart and the nurses followed his orders strictly allowing James to only suck ice chips. His lungs were still congested and they re-introduced breathing treatments every four hours.

On day three James developed a low-grade fever, his lungs filled with secretions and the breathing treatments and back-tapping intensified. He refused to smile or talk and despised the mandatory coughing because it tortured his sensitive incisions. Poor little guy. He looked miserable.

I leaned against his bed and prayed, "Father, I plead again for James. I ask you specifically to help his lungs to clear. Please protect him from pneumonia and any other infections. Give him the strength he needs to cough. Protect him from rejection, Lord. Help the medications to work so his body does not suffer rejection. Lord, you have begun a great healing in James. I trust you to complete your work."

Saturday, January 24, 1998, 8 a.m.

Father,

I praise you today. I lift my voice to sing praises to the King – the Sovereign Lord who rules, reigns and provides. I know you as Jehovah Jirah, my provider. Like Abraham of old, we laid James on your altar. You could have taken him home, for he belongs to you, but you chose instead to return him to us like Isaac back to Abraham. We rejoice at your faithfulness to us.

I think I might know how Jairus felt. I called you, pleaded with you for mercy, and you came and said, "He's only sleeping. Let me raise him up for you." Like Lazarus in the tomb, you waited before you performed your miracle. You asked us to wait for your perfect timing.

Guard my heart from fear. Keep my mind focused on you. Fix my eyes on you, walking on the water. Let me not look at the waves crashing around me so that I sink like Peter.

Lord, as I would open your word, I ask for your righteous right hand to feed me. I come to your banquet table like a hungry waif. I look to you to nourish my soul, feed my spirit and fill my mind with yourself.

In the afternoon Kathy and Souhila called. "Lizzie, we went to Veray's viewing yesterday and her funeral today. We met her mom, Donna. We were scared, didn't know what to say, if we were crossing a line we shouldn't be near. We remembered the hospital strongly discouraged contact with the donor family. But we just had to go. We knew we had to go."

They were on two extensions, talking excitedly in stereo.

"We entered the funeral home very fearful. We didn't know a soul. We had prayed the whole way there for God to show us what to do, what to say. The first lady to approach us was Donna. She thought we were co-workers from her mom's office. We commented on the pin on her lapel which read, "In their final hour, they gave a lifetime." Donna reached into her pocket and pulled out a tiny sheet of paper. Lizzie, it was a list of all Veray's organs that had been sent to Shands and who had received them. When she reached the line which read four-year-old boy – heart, we looked into each other's eyes. This was the opening we had prayed for. We whispered, "Donna, Veray's heart has been given to our nephew, James.""

"What did she do then?" I asked.

"She screamed, out loud, right there in the funeral home. Then she motioned for all her family members to come over. She repeated to everyone, "Their nephew was the one who got Veray's heart." Lizzie, you're going to love her. She's warm and loving. She's Italian and looks exactly like we do. We could be sisters.""

But we were sisters now, joined not at the hip but the heart. I already loved this brave lady. I loved her for looking beyond her tragedy and desiring to bring some good out of great sorrow. I admired her for being selfless when it would have been easy to bury herself in her own pain. She was forced to make a difficult choice. Knowing her daughter was brain-dead and that nothing more medically could be done for her, she listened to counsel from a procurement nurse at Broward General and made the greatest sacrifice possible. She could have walked away, shaking her head no. She chose instead to share Veray's viable, healthy organs. What love! What selfless love.

I would learn later that while I was signing one terrifying consent form after another prior to the transplant surgery, Donna had just completed placing her signature on dozens of consent forms as well. I was signing to accept a transplanted heart on behalf of my son; she had to sign consent forms giving approval for them to take her daughter's organs away.

Kathy and Souhila had much more to share. "Today at the funeral, Donna spoke so lovingly about Veray. Everyone said she was the sweetest little girl. Donna also directed kind, gentle comments to her older daughter as well. She handled herself with such dignity and strength. We were amazed. And then, at the very end of Veray's eulogy, Donna held up the picture of James we had given her yesterday. She told the entire congregation of 300 plus people that this little boy received Veray's heart. She asked all of them to pray for his continued healing."

"Wow! This is unbelievable! How can this even be happening?"

"I have Donna's phone number," Souhila finished. "You can call her when you're ready."

We chatted for the longest while and when I finally hung up the phone, I sat still and talked to the Lord. "Father, as you see fit, allow us to help this family in any possible way through their grief."

Sunday was the fifth day post-transplant and I felt as edgy as a cat imprisoned in a cage. This place was unnatural and stifling. The machines, tubes, masks, and medications were all irritating reminders of endless days ahead. I wanted to sprint away, far away, with James in tow. The bright spot was looking at James. His skin glowed, his eyes laughed, his smile returned. The medical team continued weaning him off one medication after another but they never gave the impression we were out of the woods. So many things could go awry, so many delicate, tight-rope balancing acts to maneuver through. For one thing, the sinus node in the new heart was damaged when the heart was chilled for transfer. This might mean another pacemaker. New heart, same problem. How odd!

Kelli's comments later were also odd. James tested positive for having immunities to chicken pox, mononucleosis and herpes simplex (cold sores). For an immune suppressed patient, viral infections are particularly dangerous. Somehow, God had allowed James to be exposed to various viruses prior to his transplant which allowed his body to build up immunities to a host of possible illnesses. I could not recall him ever having chicken pox or mononucleosis and celebrated that he would never have to fight those battles.

He would have many other battles to fight, however, if I believed everything listed in the blue manual Kelli Harker handed me. The photocopied notebook was entitled *Pediatric Cardiac Transplant Program Patient Handbook* and was written and published by the Children's Hospital at Shands, University of Florida, Pediatric Transplant Team. The handbook informed me, for one thing, that his body might recognize the new heart as an antigen or a foreign living object. If the body reacted to the transplanted heart this way it would manufacture specific cells to fight the antigen, called antibodies. The T-cell or lymphocyte was a special white blood cell which the body would produce to mistakenly attack the new heart. In order to prevent this problem, James' own immune system had to be suppressed to prevent the formation of antibodies that would cause rejection. Suppression of his immune system, or immunosuppression, would be accomplished with medications, some of which he would need to take every day for the rest of his life.

Cyclosporine was the immunosuppressant Dr. Fricker chose for James, and it worked by inhibiting the effectiveness of the T-cells in the immune system. The medication would be given in liquid form since James was too young to swallow capsules. Kelli brought a sample of the cyclosporine to the room and taught me how to carefully pull up the medication in a glass syringe. The immunosuppressant was such a powerful liquid it would eat through plastic.

James' new heart also required a steroid to prevent rejection, and he was placed on Prednisone. This medication would give James a rounded face, weight gain and an increased appetite. In addition to his daily dose of the steroid, Prednisone would also be prescribed to treat an episode of mild rejection. High doses of Prednisone would be administered for several days and then the dose would be rapidly decreased. For moderate episodes of rejection, Solu-Medrol, the intravenous form of Prednisone, would be used. To treat moderate to severe rejection, a 10 to 14 day hospitalization would be required, while Atgam or other powerful anti-rejection medications would be administered intravenously.

The diagnosis of rejection after a heart transplant would be determined by Dr. Fricker and his team based on the results of an endomyocardial biopsy performed during a heart catheterization. During the biopsy a minute piece of heart tissue, about the size of a bread crumb, would be taken for examination under a microscope. The first biopsy would be performed two weeks after the transplant surgery, and subsequent biopsies would be conducted every two weeks for about a two month period. For the first year after his transplant, James would have to undergo a biopsy every three months. The interval between biopsies would then be determined by James' condition and the fact that the likelihood of rejection decreased over time.

The written manual explained that Dr. Fricker and his staff would perform the biopsy in the cardiac catheterization lab where they would first sedate James. They would enter his body at the right side of his neck and place a small tube in the neck vein. A special instrument would be threaded through the tube, passed further down the vein and into the right ventricle of the heart. The minute heart tissue samples would be sent to pathology for examination to determine any signs of rejection.

During the biopsy procedure, Dr. Fricker would measure the blood pressure in the right side of the heart and also measure how well the heart was pumping. These additional measurements were alternatives to discover whether there were any possibilities of impending rejection. Biopsies were graded according to the degree of rejection seen when the heart tissue was examined. The number of lymphocytes exposed and the damage, if any, they rendered the heart muscle decided the grade of rejection of the biopsy.

A zero grade was the best possible outcome of a biopsy, for it would signify absolutely no rejection whatsoever. A 1A or 1B grade would mean mild rejection and a 2 would announce moderate rejection in one area of tissue. A grade of 3A or 3B would signify moderate rejection in more than one area of tissue. I never wanted the result to be a grade of 4, either. This would mean severe rejection of the transplanted heart. Definitely not a battle I wanted James to be remotely involved with!

Neither was I thrilled with him having to face infections from bacteria and viruses because of the immunosuppressant medications.

But we had no choice. This tightrope balancing act was one we had signed up for when we agreed to the transplant. It simply came with the territory. But there were ways of limiting and even preventing infections. For one thing, James would always be in a private room while in the hospital. Visitors would be limited and systematic hand washing greatly encouraged. He would be forced to wear a mask whenever he left the room for any length of time, and he could walk the halls for exercise only during low traffic periods in the evenings and early morning hours. Naturally, his temperature, heart rate and blood samples would quickly draw attention to any possible infections.

James would be treated with medications to help eliminate infections as well. Because he would be prone to thrush, a fungal infection in the mouth, James would have to swish, but not swallow, an antifungal liquid called Nystatin before bedtime. He would also receive the antibiotic Bactrim three days a week to prevent the lung infection called pneumocystitis carnii. Once we were allowed to return home, we would have to rule out infections by immediately notifying the Shands team if we noticed a persistent cough, a fever above 101, persistent colds or flu-like symptoms, increased tiredness or generalized weakness or loss of appetite. They warned us to be aware of redness, swelling or drainage around any of his incisions and for chills or night sweats. Did he have an ear ache, was he experiencing burning when he urinated or did he have a scratchy or sore throat? The transplant team wanted to be made aware of any of these symptoms.

We would have to purchase a pediatric size blood pressure kit and record his blood pressure numbers every day. To ensure James did not develop an irregular heart beat, I would also need to record his pulse daily.

This transplant business was not for the faint of heart.

CHAPTER 14

TIE A YELLOW RIBBON

"I will rejoice to the LORD, and I will be joyful to my God."
-James' Journal Entry, October 5, 2004

INALLY, after four intense weeks in Gainesville, after one last biopsy reported a zero rejection count, after one more round of release forms and lessons in administering the large doses of medications, we loaded our red Aerostar van, slammed the apartment door shut, and drove away triumphantly. Like Lance Armstrong looping around Les Champs - Elysees in Paris after winning the Tour de' France, we did our victory lap on the Turnpike and swung towards home.

Yellow ribbons and bright yellow streamers beamed from every palm and shade tree that lined the main street of our subdivision, while brilliant red heart-shaped balloons swirled from mail boxes and sailed from the tips of children's fingers. I slowed the van, tears obstructing my view of dozens of neighbors, family and friends standing on both sides of the street while reporters with their camera crews stood in front of our home. The triumphant soldier was receiving his victory parade, and his dad straddled the middle of the road, arms outstretched, face brightly lit. Our family was safely home.

"Welcome Home," announced piles of presents, stacks of cards and delicious meals covering the kitchen countertop. "Welcome Home," echoed loving family and helpful friends. "Welcome Home," screamed clean sheets on our clean bed, our own bed. Good to be home, great to be home, at last. We savored our first night, James sleeping soundly in our bedroom, all six of us finally under our own roof again.

As a tribute to the Lord and a grateful proclamation to all who had accompanied us on this part of the journey, we composed another poem and mailed it along with a bright picture of James, his face chubby from steroids.

JAMESONG

Deep in the shadows where voices sound grim
The unknown screams loudly, calamity rings
Heartache trades places with icy, cold fear
Terror sows anguish, souls cry despair.
Our brave one is failing, the warrior's worn down,
Flung from the saddle, knocked to the ground
Helpless we hold him, heart torn and frail
Waiting while watching for God's answered prayer.
Then over the bedlam a melody flies
Brighter than smiles from James' twinkling eyes
Drowning out chaos, it carries a tune
Listen - each note sounds to wash away gloom.
Rest in the conflict, Almighty is near
Abandon your burdens into His care
Higher than heaven, broader that seas,
Wider His love than ten galaxies.
Strength for the struggle, no matter how long
Hope to wipe anguish out of the song
Peace like a banner, courage the band
Aid to endure, all gifts from His hand.
Hundreds surround us like armies of old
They come to help conquer fear's ugly hold
With arm loads of comfort each carries our pain

Renewing and soothing us time and again.
Their mercy like music echoes, refills
Voices speak courage, love flows and spills
Kind gentle measures like soothing, old hymns
Splashing refreshment on worn, weary limbs.
Slits in the shadow, see the boy rise
Victory in battle, God returns our sweet prize
In wonder we watch him regain and recharge
Beyond expectation we soar with the stars.
Laughter is far flung and joy plays her verse
Peace the main chorus from God's perfect voice
Our Father in Heaven who dwells among men
Envelopes his children, strengthening them
To face life's rough waters and storm's noisy gales
But He never forsakes and He never fails.

I longed to contact Donna Caridi to thank her for the enormous role she had played in James' life and recovery, but I was completely sapped physically and emotionally. In time I would connect with our donor family, but for now we spent every ounce of energy managing James and his new routines. We were a household gripped with coping with a newly transplanted patient and the regiment of administering medications, monitoring blood pressure and watching James closely for any signs of rejection while attempting to care for all the regular needs of a family of six. Gradually, we settled into a routine, a new norm, and the overwhelming adjustments became common place.

Every few weeks we returned to Gainesville for those dreaded biopsies, but we never tired of hearing a "zero" report. James experienced the smallest possible levels of rejection, his new heart was behaving like a perfect match. On March 23, 1998, I awoke to the wonderful reality of celebrating James' fifth birthday. Our son was alive. Our son was well. In His mercy, in His graciousness, God had given James a brand new life.

In the afternoon, with trembling hands, I dialed Donna Caridi's number. "Donna, this is Elizabeth Mitchell. I'm James' mom."

"How's he doing?" the gentle voice on the line responded.

"He's well. His heart's doing incredibly well. The doctor's are all thrilled. We are getting great results on all his biopsies. He's hardly had any rejection at all."

"Oh, I'm so glad." Donna's voice, though sweet, held sadness in each word.

"Donna, I need to thank you," I continued. "I must let you know how grateful we are for what you did for our family. We really want to thank you. You were incredibly brave to make such a difficult decision."

"I wish there could have been some other way…some other way." Her voice shook.

I swallowed hard. I swallowed again. "Donna, I wish there could have been some other way, too."

Silence hung between us for a while.

We exchanged addresses, and I promptly sent her pictures of James and kept in touch periodically. I longed to meet this courageous, loving woman in person and finally at the beginning of May picked up the phone and invited her to our home. The following Sunday would work. She could come over in the afternoon. Wonderful! It was all set. I put down the phone and turned to write the date on the calendar. Sunday would be Mother's Day.

Mother's Day, when her heart would be carrying an empty, aching load, they rang the doorbell and stepped timidly into our home, strangers intricately intertwined inside our lives. We hugged, held tightly, and then introduced our children to each other. She was warm, easy to talk with, loving. When we played card games in the family room, James ended up on Donna's team and nestled close to her. She had been on his team since January 20th.

After we had munched cookies Bill corralled all the kids and headed to the basketball hoop outside. The silence gave the two of us permission to share details of Veray's death, of Donna's and her older daughter's walk through sorrow, of how they coped with their grief. We stood after a long while. We were not strangers anymore.

The children filtered back into the house slowly. James came into the kitchen as we were heading to the front door and I picked him up and plopped him on the kitchen counter. Without contemplating the thought too long I said, "Donna, would you like to listen to his heart?"

She nodded, bent her head toward his chest and pressed her ear against his heart. She lingered there for quite a while. No one spoke, the children stood in a hushed silence behind us. They knew we stood on Holy Ground. James sat perfectly still. Time stopped.

CHAPTER 15

NO TIME FOR FAREWELLS

"One day I will see the Lord face to face and the one whom the Lord sees face to face is in heaven."
— *James' Journal Entry, March 4, 2005*

THE truth is, all his suffering only made him sweeter. Multiple incisions from the surgeries scarred his chest and his breast bone was crooked and deformed from having been hacked through and bound back. The pacemaker protruded through his skinny torso and his neck was marked by the dozens of invasive biopsies that wove through the vein to his heart. But like a gentle lamb, brought to be shorn over and over, the marks never marked him, never made him ill-tempered or sour-faced or sensitive or selfish. Rather, in some miraculous way, the suffering, the annoying medications, the periodic, routine biopsies, the probing and questioning and monitoring and scrutiny only softened, sweetened, tenderized his impressionable soul.

He was not a broken horse, lassoed to his troubles, but instead he was a stallion, strong, fast, and secure. He raced unbridled, the meadow winds pouring through his mane, sweat foaming at his nostrils, a champion at every turn. James attacked life, in whatever shape it came. Passion poured from every nerve ending he possessed. It was as if he knew, even as a little boy, that life itself was a magical, miraculous, extra-ordinary gift, and he could not waste one moment on anything less than celebration. He laughed intensely and cheered for others at the top of his lungs. He played hard, studied with diligence and captured the meaning of why God had left him on earth, running to the finish line, fully spent, every ounce given to the grand cause of bringing glory to the Father, who had on more occasions than he could possibly know, spared his life for some great task ahead.

He fidgeted uncomfortably whenever Bill or I shared his story in public. He disliked being the illustration in my talks or Bill's sermons. I was convinced he would eventually accomplish greatness in athletics, in medicine, or perhaps in ministry, standing before large audiences and testifying to God's miraculous, supernatural work on his behalf. He was packed tight with potential and bubbled over with enthusiasm, diligence, and zeal. He poured it all out on memorizing Scripture, writing stories, drawing sketches, painting watercolors and reading biographies of great men and women of faith.

James was all about whistling in the shower, singing with gusto, winning computer games, dribbling down the court, making three point shots, cheering his teammates, squeezing his sister, tackling his cousins in football, smashing the ping-pong ball to his dad, riding a bike, jumping on the trampoline, working with his math tutor, munching popcorn in front of a televised sporting event, playing with babies, teaching kids Bible verses and meticulously completing his chores. He lived life large, lived life well, flew down the track, won the race, arrived there first, went in ahead - far too soon it seemed to me.

He defied all the medical odds. The blue transplant manual was inaccurate from his perspective. The team at Shands took every opportunity to investigate offensively and examine him meticulously in order to ward off rejection. We returned to Gainesville faithfully, holding our breath as they probed and questioned. The transplant team vigilantly searched for the faintest signs of rejection, anything that would clue them to the slightest cardiac malfunction. Eventually, when all his results were negative, they labeled him "medically boring" and continued their attentive oversight anyway.

"Call us if you notice anything unusual," they cautioned.

But I rarely found it necessary. His immune system was compromised because of the immune-suppressant medications he swallowed twice daily, and, naturally, he should be susceptible to viruses and bacteria. But he hardly even picked up a cold, let alone an infection. We monitored his medications, poured them in a small white dish on the kitchen counter, and when he could stop playing, eating, or laughing long enough, he would plop them all in his mouth, all eight or nine tablets, every day, without complaining or whining or wondering why he had to be different and swallow stuff and put up with annoying rituals.

He simply took his bumps with style, never drew attention to himself, never realized it was a big deal that his heart had not started out as his own. He made it his own. He had more heart than most people ever dream of having. It pumped love, passion, joy and gentleness into every moment he lived. He came to demonstrate that regardless of the bruises, the challenges, the hurdles, a person should run fast, grin cheerfully, play intensely, give all, reserve nothing for tomorrow, encourage everyone in one's path, look out for the weak, turn life into a fast-paced joy ride, and give love extravagantly everywhere one happens to go.

And then, before we could say good-bye, while he was still racing round the track, full-speed, no reigning in, the eternal gates opened, beckoned him, and he galloped through, stalling long enough for us to see his tail waving in the wind, to glimpse the breeze blowing through his mane as he flew inside. He never looked back; he never had to. He had no regrets. He had spent every moment of life bringing joy and pleasure simply with his exuberant presence, brilliant smile, tender voice and boundless, limitless energy.

So, when the Father called from across the valley, when he beckoned him to leave his weary, worn out heart behind and come to the place of immortality, he followed. He had walked closely with his Creator and knew the Shepherd's voice. He had listened closely to the sound in solitary places when he rose early, even on summer days, to prop himself in the corner of the couch or in between neatly tucked sheets of his bed to read his Bible.

He had heard his Savior's call from the moment he handed himself completely over to Him at five years of age until the middle of his thirteenth year, when the Savior beckoned, "Come quickly now. You've done your part. You've finished the job I sent you to perform. You've shown them what a life lived in love with me looks like. You have demonstrated that a struggle need not strangle joy but rather can strengthen it until a harvest of beauty grows precisely from the soil of the suffering. You lived a life so filled with me that wherever I sent you, whatever hospital housed you, surgeon sliced you, doctor probed you, nurse monitored you, family member held you, teacher listened to you, friend played with you, teammate heard you, they all knew you to be different because I crafted you for a different purpose. I created you to show anyone willing to discern that adversity never conquers the soul I fill with my Spirit, that challenges knock off selfishness in hearts tuned into me, that pain produces power in the weakest containers, that joy is born in places full of sorrow, that laughter is sweeter when mined in fields of tears, that passion for me and for my word produces giants others see as little boys.

"Let them see, dearest boy, that I make all things new, that no difficult place is purposeless, that trials tenderize and peel away the natural stains so that my brilliant light can shine through. Let them understand from you that fruit grown in orchards of adversity is sweeter to the taste and more beautiful to the eye. Let them hear in your voice that gladness comes from sorrow, that enthusiasm and an unconquerable spirit flow from the places we never want to go. Let them watch you closely now, for when I call you home they will remember you as living life as I intended.

The road I sent you on cost you dearly, but I allowed it for a purpose. I will not allow you to suffer more harm. Come home, my boy, come home."

And because He made him to be a fighter, a warrior to overcome and compensate and survive endless hardships, James fought bravely even at the end. "Mom, I cannot wait to have a glass of ice-cold milk," he said to me after vomiting again. He leaned against the doorframe, slumped into our bed and his very last words were, "Mom, help me. I can't breathe."

For just a few passing moments, long enough for those who loved him best of all to come close and gather by his side, he fought valiantly once more. But the Father's call was stronger yet and when his weeping earthly father whispered in his ear, "Go home, son. Your Heavenly Father is calling you. Go home, sweet boy. You've done well. Don't struggle any more," he listened in obedience and flew.

The brave soldier needed to fight no more wars.

CHAPTER 16

YOU DO THE NEXT THING

"God doesn't want us to be grumpy when we have a trial. He wants us to have faith and joy in every trial."
— *James' Journal Entry, February 23, 2006*

BUT we must. Our war rages on.

Slumped in a metal chair on August 17, 2006, right outside the door where James' lifeless body lay, surrounded by a hundred weeping souls, I asked Bill, "What do we do now? We've never been here before. How will we make it through?"

I quickly found out the answer to my questions. Elizabeth Elliot says, "You simply do the next thing." You sit and cry on the very couch where you once played a game. You stand in your closet and ask yourself, "What do I wear to plan my son's funeral?" and then you pull on dark clothes, for anything with color seems vulgar. You plead with God for the grace to see your child in a coffin and He gives you strength to view the precious body that you know, is just a shell. James no longer lives there. He is someplace grand and glorious, and you press on.

You plan the pieces of the service, dress yourself, stand in a line beside the casket, talk and smile and cry. You feel the prayers of God's people wrapped around you like mighty, reinforced steel, and you are incapable of collapsing for the armor holds you steady, the Father holds you upright.

You walk behind the casket, and breathing becomes hard. Tight hands squeeze your lungs, intense pressure mounts where once a regular heart beat. The world as you knew it is no more, no more cadence or order. All gone, swept into that tiny box they ease into a hole. Roses drape the coffin; sorrow drapes everything else.

But I do the next thing. I listen to others talking, feel their arms, hear their words of kindness, but always I am out of sync. James left a gigantic hole behind him, and I simply keep falling in. I wake in the morning and hold my husband tight, tighter than I ever have before, and we fill the room with memories, retelling, reliving, reciting the brilliance that is no more. But I must place my feet on the floor, take a step, do the next thing.

Music soothes and reaches places I never knew existed. Books bring words to focus on, follow and have somewhat of a plan. But mostly I cry. People envelope me with gentle, tender acts of kindness; the smallest bouquet is a gorgeous meadow displaying the Creator's tranquil beauty. Each written note, each call, blows a speck of hopelessness out the door. Grief-bearers come in many forms.

But mostly I hide in the shelter of wings far greater than my own. The night calls my name and I rise to meet my Savior in His Word. He is my Kinsman-Redeemer, covering me with his garments and saying in a hundred ways, "And now, my daughter, don't be afraid. I will do for you all you ask" (Ruth 3:11). In the morning light I ask for more, more grace, more mercy, more help. I press my face against green carpet inside my darkened closet, desperate, anxious, trembling. I bring Him a soul ravaged and scraped clean, a heart shredded into jagged pieces, a sense of being lost, a mind muddled and confused. He brings me Himself. He is always more than enough and yet I ask Him for more still.

"Father," I cry on my face, "I need nothing more than more of you. Bring the sweetness of your presence, bring your very self, and pour your perfect Holy Spirit into all the empty places you can find. I want more of You. Nothing else will satisfy."

And He comes to find me and fill me in a hundred different places. And He understands my pain. I need not be brave with Him. I need not pretend all is right. He gives me permission to grieve with every nerve, every cell, every fiber of every single part of me. He knitted James inside my womb. He glued him to my soul when He asked me to walk with him through 13 years of struggle. He forged an inseparable alliance between us when he made him our son. And now He understands the ripping apart, the agony of separation, the intense longing to hold him, touch him, see him. He placed a treasure in our hands, knowing the treasure would become invaluable and that when He relinquished us from the task, the lost treasure would leave a gaping wound..

For 13 years, God deflected the arrow of death as it sailed toward us, bloody and putrid, intent on causing havoc. He prevented it from penetrating our hearts – this close you may come, but no further. Four or five times he grabbed the point right before it punctured, but this time He kept his hands to His side as death found its intended target, stealing James, slicing us into a thousand miserable pieces. And though I long for healing from the arrow's wound, he leaves the tip within. I feel it with each move.

And yet, knowing the cost, I would do it all again. I heard of a mother recently who discovered cardiac malfunction in her child and coped with her dilemma by choosing an abortion. Immediately, I blurted out, "She threw away a James," and pitied her for discarding the opportunity to live with precious cargo. What a foolish woman. How she would grieve one day to know what she missed and could never regain. How kind and good my Father was to entrust James into our care and give us the privilege of living with a remarkable boy who came to teach us lessons we could learn no other way.

As a family God instructed us to travel to a rugged mission field requiring sacrifice and surrender, a land filled with difficult terrain and impossible challenges, where our strenuous efforts would often yield an uncertain outcome. But fully convinced that this was his prepared will for us, we abandoned comfort and ease and paid the price to fulfill the calling to care for James.

But then the mission field was altered, replaced with the lands of sorrow, separation and unending loss. He beckoned us to live in a valley of tears and longings and aching, to surrender and embrace this new place. Would He not also provide for us here? Would we not have His certain presence, empowerment, enabling, the sweetness of His very self at this juncture of our perilous journey, even though it lie far, far away from any plan of ours.

Since I am called to this battle, I must prepare for hardship and struggle and not expect an easy road, comfortable paths or cheerful days. I must be ready for rugged fights, long treacherous nights, heat and grime and total inconvenience of every kind. Would my Commander send me where He has not first fought, lay down his life on my account, providing now all the necessary weapons for me to come through victorious? As He leads, I must follow.

Is sorrow not like that great fish that swallowed Jonah whole, the scary unknown that God used to rescue Jonah and bring him to a place of ministry? The fish that Jonah feared as it opened horrendous jaws and imprisoned him in a black and dreadful hole was God's hand-crafted provision for him to escape the storm and arrive safely where God intended him to serve. Is sorrow that sort of fish for us?

Grief comes like a den of hungry lions, waiting to sink their teeth into our necks, breaking every bone. But like Daniel of old, I watch God shut sorrow's gaping jaw; He will not allow it to devour and destroy.

Somewhat like Joseph, I have been kidnapped, thrown into a pit and sold into bondage in Egypt. I am now a slave in this strange land and I must still serve my Lord here, especially here. *Father, I pray you would allow me to know the favor of Joseph, the sweetness of your presence resting on me in this foreign place as I linger and labor here for you.*

Beauty for ashes is His promise. My ashes are burnt remains of dreams and hopes and wholeness, scars and wounds and gashes inflicted by this intense season in the furnace of pain. *Here Father, I exchange all these with you. I give you my ashes. May your beauty be seen in me.*

Epilogue—
August 2008

"God wants us to speak the truth and tell other people about Jesus."

-James' Journal Entry October 29, 2004

AMES' face lies hidden from my view; his gaze takes in the face of God. The voice which I knew once, whose cry drew me quickly in response, I can no longer hear, no matter how hard I strain. But God himself now speaks his name, beckons him, and communicates with my dear son, with His dear one. Though my fingertips fail to touch his tender skin or grasp his hand, he reaches now to touch beyond the hem of the garment of the Son of God. I lack the pleasure of his company but he enjoys the friendship of the saints, heroes we only know by printed page and faded photographs. James no longer occupies our home, our table, our life, but in heaven he worships with Abraham of old, fearless Joshua, courageous Esther and trusting Mary. Why would I ever bid him return or deprive him of celestial life in exchange for the ordinary, sweaty tears of earth?

With the perspective of time, I realize that while our family was spiraling into the "dark night of the soul", James was entering his most brilliant morning. While night descended in its blackest form, daylight shone brighter for James than it ever had before. As we were weeping in anguish, forlorn and downcast on every side, our young boy was encountering a level of indescribable joy.

While right before our eyes we were forced to watch him slip away, his spectacular life was only just beginning. As his body lay naked on that emergency room table, EKG leads stuck to his broken hearted chest, James was entering heaven fully clothed in the Lord's righteousness. In the surreal moments of farewell, in that sterile stainless steel hospital cell, James entered the land where sorrow cannot go, where tears are banished and pain is barred all entry. As we reluctantly loosened our grip on our son, the Lord had already tightened his hold on him. While we slumped, completely dismayed, for the very first time in all his life James stood completely whole.

Despite such brilliant, eternal considerations, I still long for his presence in our family, still ache for the insurmountable loss we incurred. I weep often for the boy I will never know, the man who will never be. But our son belongs to a different place in God's realm and lives where time cannot bring him pain, where the morning brings no news of trouble or toil ahead. He does not pine for earth any more than an infant longs to return to the unlit, cramped womb from which he came. The phrase, "James died" falsifies his present condition for now he lives as he never has before. Now he tastes the cup of life and finds the richness of the flavor immense and satisfying. He knows no lack of strength, no timid days, no fearful nights. Wrapped in the blanket of heaven, he rests perfectly content, secure, and constantly aware of the presence of Almighty God and the beauty of His holiness.

I celebrate for James.

I watch his brother graduate, buy a car, find a job and pursue a godly wife and rejoice at his many accomplishments. Should I not cheer louder still for James' glorious position where cap and gown and wedding band pale in comparison, where he holds job security forever and perfect, unconditional love surrounds his every move? He reclines now at a sumptuous table with his Lord. What sparse festivities is he exactly missing here?

If I could, I would ask him now, "Are you in a place, dear one, where animals talk and the Lion of Judah holds court? Have you chatted with all those heroes you read about in riveting biographies and glimpsed the faces of the Bible greats who walked across the pages of Scripture when once we snuggled close? Have you questioned Jonah about his fish-belly prison or has Daniel mentioned what it felt like to pillow his head on a lion's mane? Has David showed you how he slung that stone and let you carefully finger Goliath's enormous sword?

Does Moses call your name? Does Abraham take walks with you? Does Paul whisper tales into your ear and Peter help you understand how awesome was the sight of Christ risen from the grave? How beautiful is Esther? Is Ruth indeed so kind? And how amazing is it, son of mine, to look into the eyes of Christ and drink in the love reflected there?

Do you now understand why I loved my precious mother and why I longed for you to know her too? Is she lovelier than the pictures on our wall? Was she the first to meet you as you entered heaven's door? Did you fall asleep in one grandmother's arms on earth and wake wide-eyed in hers?

Do you pal around with Uncle Steve like Daddy used to do? Are you the best of friends on adventures that make all their escapades on earth seem timid and plain? Do they let you know how you are missed and how often we call your name? Is there a meter measuring how grateful we are that we ever got to know you and love you well?

Is it a wonder to wear no scars and never feel a pain? How incredible for you that God took you fast, for you never knew your heart was failing here. How kind he is to graciously spare you life's greatest sorrow. He asked you to endure trials and grievous calamities but he spared you from mourning the loss of a love you held dear. I am glad, my boy, you never knew this pain.

*   *   *

If given a choice, I would have chosen to finish James' story differently. Somehow, with my finite capabilities, I would have scripted him a spectacular leading role, center stage, triumphant and victorious, despite the odds stacked against him. He would have made a brilliant heart surgeon. That was his plan, to help other children as he had been helped. Sounded like a lovely plan to me.

But I bow my will to the perfect will of God. I need not understand or comprehend his choices but I stand fully convinced that I serve a God completely trustworthy. He has proven himself faithful and I fix my eyes on the one who makes all things new. He owes me no explanation. He sent me on a journey for the heart and provided himself as my constant companion through thirteen years of James' life and two strenuous years of mourning his death. The journey never failed to be extraordinary. With every step our amazing God traveled by my side. He has no plans to abandon me now.

"With my mouth I will make your faithfulness known through all generations. I will declare that your love stands firm forever, that you established your faithfulness in heaven itself" (Psalm 89:1b-2).

APPENDIX

What to Grab Before You Dash to the Emergency Room or What to Ask a Friend to Bring For You

- Cell phone (hopefully programmed with pertinent telephone numbers).
- Insurance Cards.
- List of medications and known drug allergies.
- Photo I.D.
- Wallet.
- Phone numbers of physicians and specialists.
- Favorite blanket, pillow, stuffed toy for child.
- Light sweater or jacket. (Hospitals are notoriously cold and fear always makes you feel colder.)

What to Do While Waiting In the Emergency Room

- Call a friend who will mobilize others to pray. Give a specific request.
- Jot down questions for the attending physician.
- Think carefully of pertinent information and medical history you should relay to emergency room staff.
- Take a few deep breaths.
- Ask God to give you His grace and peace to handle what lies ahead.

Specific Steps to Prevent Crises from Crushing You

- Pray
- Call friends to pray for/with you
- When you can't pray because you are overwhelmed, simply repeat the prayer, "Jesus, help me." He will.
- Hide in the Psalms – keep your Bible nearby and read even one verse and allow your mind to dwell on that one promise, one thought from God's Word. Wrap your emotions of fear, anxiety, and panic inside the strong arms of Scripture.
- Ask those who stand beside you, call you on the phone or sit next to you to read the Scriptures aloud in order to focus your mind on God's powerful Word.
- Speak your fears aloud. Share them with your spouse or a good friend who knows how to listen.
- Journal your deepest concerns and fears.
- Slip away from the crises and take a walk. Squeeze in exercise somehow.
- Listen to Praise and Worship music.
- Allow yourself to cry. Tears release tension.
- Make a list of everything you can be thankful for and thank God for them.
- Allow people to serve you, help you, and care for you. If they ask, "What can I do to help?" give them some specific task that would help you. Receive the gift of their love and know you will have the chance to serve others another day.

Essential Items for an Extended Hospital Stay with Your Loved One

- Comfortable clothes like sweat pants and tops that you can both sleep in and be seen in public. Very little privacy occurs in hospital corridors.

- Extremely comfortable shoes. You are on your feet on very hard flooring at all hours of the day and night.
- Sweater or jacket. Hospitals are always cooler than the outside world.
- Compact toiletry bag. Preferable one that hangs on a hook. Vanity space is non-existent in hospital lavatories.
- Bible. Essential for warding off fear, anxiety and endless waiting.
- Journal and some pens. You don't want to forget what God is teaching you in this undesirable classroom and you might easily misplace one pen.
- Cheerful family photograph to prop beside the patient's bed so the medical staff can visualize the real person inside that generic hospital gown and treat them accordingly.
- Socks. Never walk barefoot anywhere in a hospital.
- List of phone numbers of favorite people for sharing the difficult days and the good reports as well.
- Healthy snacks. The vending machine's chocolate bars and potato chips will never get you through this grueling adventure camp.
- Your own medications and vitamins. You must stay healthy too.
- An Ipod or Compact CD player with Praise and Worship CD's. Reality TV will give you nothing to help you cope with your present reality. Tune out the noise and turn up the praise. Your sanity may very well depend on it.
- A spiral notebook for jotting phone messages, items needed from home and questions and concerns you want to mention to the nurses and doctors.

Survival Essentials for Entertaining Pediatric Patients

- Special blanket, pillow and/or stuffed toy – security comes in all shapes and textures.
- Small photo album stuffed with favorite family photographs.
- Pack of playing cards – perfect for dealing out a quick game of "Go Fish" or "Old Maid" right on the hospital bed. Can be quickly packed away when suddenly interrupted by nurses and easily replaced if left behind in waiting rooms.
- Familiar old books and a few brand new ones, as well.
- Sticker album with assorted stickers.
- Travel-size games like Connect 4 and Monopoly.
- Erasable writing board.
- Disposable camera for the patient to click goofy shots of his visitors.
- A "Piggy Bank" so the patient can extract a toll from every therapist, doctor or visitor who crosses the threshold of his room.
- A portable tape recorder with tapes from family and friends sending greetings, telling jokes, sharing a Bible verse, or relating a funny story. Request these cassettes as gifts from far away family and friends asking what they can do to help.
- Postcards already stamped and pre-addressed to family members or school friends for her to write a short note or simply to print her name before giving to someone to mail.
- Colorful posters to hang on those sterile hospital walls.

How to Help a Friend Navigate Through an Emergency

- Dispense hugs generously.
- Dispense advice sparingly.
- Listen without interrupting with your own story.
- Organize meals for the family at home.
- Bring a delicious wrapped sandwich or salad to the hospital.

- Time stands still in waiting rooms. Your company will help nudge the clock ahead.
- Borrow her house key and invite two other friends to help you clean and do the laundry.
- Mail an envelope stuffed with notes from the neighbors, co-workers, small group Bible study group or Sunday school class.
- Volunteer to care for the other children in the family and make their day bright with games, a special meal or a unique outing.
- Collect money to help offset unexpected expenses.
- Call and pray with her on the phone.
- Write out one meaningful Bible verse and tuck it into an encouraging note.
- Get her to smile. Do whatever it takes. Laughter is the best stress reliever.
- Gather a group of friends who will commit to fasting and prayer for a designated period.

What to Do after You Say "I'm Sorry"

- Sit quietly and listen. Your gentle presence speaks loudest. Let your words be few.
- Don't say, "Call me if you need anything." Grieving moms won't. Just show up and be useful:

> Put on a load of laundry. Fold another.
> Stack the dishwasher.
> Answer the phone. Write down the message
>   with a return number.
> Clean the bathrooms.
> Throw out old newspapers.
> Water the plants.
> Go to the store. Pick up what's missing
>   from the refrigerator.

- Send cards weeks and months after the funeral. Most people move on but grieving parents don't. Pray for them and write and tell them that you did.
- Call on the anniversary of the death. Remind them you haven't forgotten.
- Mail a package with small treats for the other siblings. A gift in the mail always brings a smile.
- Send an e-mail now and then. Keep it short. Let it be a gentle reminder of your love and genuine concern.
- Stop by unexpectedly and leave an arrangement of fresh flowers with a card at the door.
- Invite the family for dinner at your home. Keep the meal simple and the conversation kind.
- Ask the question, "Tell me all about your child. What was she like?" You could not give grieving parents a greater gift.

How to Pray for Friends Experiencing Trauma

- For God to make them keenly aware of His Presence.
- For God's Word to minister to their precise need.
- For strength to endure.
- For especially restful sleep.
- For the ability to surrender their will and accept God's will.
- For wisdom for the doctors involved.
- For the time and the desire to hide inside God's Word.
- For many people to surround them with love.
- For clear direction as decisions are being made.
- For peace to permeate every area of their lives.
- For His grace to overwhelm them.
- For them to keep their eyes fixed on what is unseen and eternal.

Highly Recommended Books to Strengthen, Comfort and Encourage

- Jerry Sittser, *A Grace Disguised: How the Soul Grows Through Loss* (Grand Rapids: Zondervan, 1995)
- Susan Drake, *Grieving Forward: Embracing Life Beyond Loss* (New York: Warner Faith, 2006)
- Anne Graham Lotz, *Why?: Trusting God When You Don't Understand* (Nashville: W Publishing Group, 2004)
- Carolyn Custis James, *When Life and Beliefs Collide: How Knowing God Makes a Difference* (Grand Rapids: Zondervan, 2001)
- Elizabeth Elliot, *A Path Through Suffering: Discovering the Relationship Between God's Mercy and Our Pain* (Ann Arbor: Servant Publications,1990)
- Margaret Clarkson, *Grace Grows Best in Winter* (Grand Rapids: Zondervan, 1972)
- Erwin Lutzer, *One Minute After You Die: A Preview of Your Final Destination* (Chicago: Moody Press, 1997)
- Nancy Guthrie, *Holding on to Hope: A pathway through suffering to the heart of God* (Wheaton: Tyndale House Publishers, Inc., 2002)
- Amy Carmichael, *Toward Jerusalem* (Fort Washington: Christian Literature Crusade, 1998)
- Frances J. Roberts, *Come Away My Beloved* (Uhrichsville: Barbour Publishing, Inc., 2002)
- Sarah Young, *Jesus Calling: Enjoying Peace in His Presence* (Nashville: Integrity Publishers, 2004)

For additional copies of *Journey for the Heart*
Log on to the website:
http://missions.awana.org
to place your order
or write to us at the address below:

O R D E R   F O R M

Please send me _____copies of Journey for the Heart
@$10 per book plus shipping and handling of $5 per book.

Please make checks payable to:
Awana International

Total Enclosed: $_____

Name:_____

Address:_____

City:_____

State/Zip_____

Please remit to:
Adopt-a-Club
Awana International
1 East Bode Road
Streamwood, IL 60107